T0248395

THE LITTLE BOOK

OF
ROBO INVESTING

Little Book Series

In the Little Book series, the brightest icons in the financial world write on topics that range from tried-and-true investment strategies to tomorrow's new trends. Each book offers a unique perspective on investing, allowing the reader to pick and choose from the very best in investment advice today.

Books in the Little Book series include:

THE LITTLE BOOK

OF
ROBO INVESTING

How to Make Money
While You Sleep

ELIZABETH MACBRIDE

QIAN LIU

WILEY

Published by John Wiley & Sons, Inc., Hoboken, New Jersey
Published simultaneously In Canada.

For general information on our other products and services or for technical support, please contact our Customer Care Department within the United States at (800) 762-2974, outside the United States at (317) 572-3993 or fax (317) 572-4002.

Wiley also publishes its books in a variety of electronic formats. Some content that appears in print may not be available in electronic formats. For more information about Wiley products, visit our web site at www.wiley.com.

Library of Congress Cataloging-in-Publication Data

Names: MacBride, Elizabeth, author.
Title: The little book of robo investing : how to make money while you
   sleep/Elizabeth Macbride, Qian Liu.
Description: Hoboken, New Jersey : Wiley, [2024] | Includes index.
Identifiers: LCCN 2023046413 (print) | LCCN 2023046414 (ebook) | ISBN
   9781394225224 (hardback) | ISBN 9781394225248 (adobe pdf) | ISBN
   9781394225231 (epub)
Subjects: LCSH: Financial services industry—Technological innovations. |
   Financial engineering.
Classification: LCC HG173 .M223 2024 (print) | LCC HG173 (ebook) | DDC
   332.10285—dc23/eng/20231103
LC record available at https://lccn.loc.gov/2023046413
LC ebook record available at https://lccn.loc.gov/2023046414

Cover Design: Paul McCarthy

SKY10063497_011124

Contents

———— ≈ ————

Foreword
By Andy Rachleff

———— ∾ ————

I MUST ADMIT I HATE the term "Robo advisor." It was conceived the first year Wealthfront offered our automated investment service, by a financial advisor who probably felt threatened by the negative impact we could have on his business. I believe he chose the term "robo" to convey something impersonal and perhaps even as annoying as marketing "robocalls."

Our clients didn't care what we were labeled in the media. They loved our service and our low fee.

Still, the knock against Robo advisors as impersonal always struck me as odd. The goal of investment management should be to maximize your return after fees and taxes have been deducted. Over the past 60 years quite a bit of research has been done to show that the only thing that matters when optimizing a portfolio for you is your tolerance for risk. An optimized portfolio gives you the best chance of a high return at a level of risk you can tolerate. As Elizabeth and Qian explain in this book, risk and return are a matched pair, a yin and yang that you can't separate. The first and only job of an advisor is to create and maintain an optimized portfolio that works for you. Everything else an advisor does can actually detract from your returns.

So I *agreed* with the many financial advisors who took to Twitter in the early days of Robo advising to make the point that Robo advisors won't be there to hold a widow's hand at her husband's funeral. Is that really what you pay a financial advisor for? As the book explains, you could be paying extraordinarily excessive fees to have someone hold your hand, and it gets even worse when you include subpar performance for focusing on the wrong issues. Most clients of traditional investment advisors don't even realize how much they're paying.

The other term associated with automated investing I hate is "algorithms." Oxford defines algorithm as "a process or set of rules to be followed in calculations or other problem-solving operations, especially by a computer." Many common definitions of Robo advising (perhaps also put about by traditional advisors) lead you to believe Robo advisors use scary algorithms that could go awry at any moment, which could lead to your portfolio taking a big loss. Many technology companies attribute their "secret sauce" to proprietary algorithms. However, there is nothing proprietary or mysterious about the algorithms Wealthfront or its competitors use. All we do is automate (meaning implement in software) the best practices of the financial advisor industry. The best practices are based on research published in the late 1950s that earned the Nobel Prize in Economics in 1990. This is perhaps the biggest reason I prefer the term "automated investing."

Over the years, Wealthfront tried to get the press and analysts to adopt "automated investing" instead of Robo advising but to no avail. They found the term Robo advising "fun" and more importantly, controversial. As a result, I have reluctantly accepted that the modifer "robo" is here to stay . . . and that this book had to be called *Little Book of Robo Investing*.

The book does a superb job of explaining why following some simple rules, based on many years of academic research can lead to far superior performance than you might expect from a traditional financial advisor. These rules can be implemented (with a lot of difficulty) manually, but the fee you pay a Robo advisor to implement them is generally covered many times over by the tax savings they are able to provide.

I never intended to found what became the largest independent Robo advisor (as of summer 2023). It happened quite by accident. After working for 21 years in the venture capital industry, including cofounding Benchmark Capital in 1995, I decided to retire in 2005. I wanted to use my retirement as an opportunity to give back for all the incredible opportunities afforded to me. I joined the faculty of my graduate school alma mater, Stanford Graduate School of Business, to teach courses on tech entrepreneurship and joined the board of trustees of my undergraduate alma mater, the University of Pennsylvania. My wife, Debbie, and I also partnered with the Damon Runyon Research Foundation to create an innovative cancer research funding initiative.

One of my trustee responsibilities was being involved with Penn's endowment investment committee, which I enjoyed. The Ivy League endowments are among the best managed diversified pools of capital in the world, and Penn's was no exception. The idea for Wealthfront came to me during a presentation by the endowment investment team on how they manage their portfolio. Coming from the world of tech entrepreneurship, I was struck by how much of their manual work could be codified into software. If someone could do that, I realized, they could make endowment-style investing accessible to everyone.

This hit a nerve, because over my many years as a venture capitalist, I was often asked for investment advice by people I recruited to my portfolio companies. I could never advise them to do what I do, because I'm in the very fortunate position of being able to afford the high minimum account sizes associated with the best investment products and services. This always struck me as wrong. Everybody needs access to high-quality investment services because it's so hard to save for a house or to retire without them.

As a seasoned venture capitalist, I knew successful companies were usually started by highly authentic entrepreneurs who took advantage of inflection points in technology to build products that served new audiences desperate for the product. Brokerage firms had recently made application programming interfaces (APIs) available. APIs enabled a fully automated investment management solution that could be combined with software to replicate most of how the Ivy League endowments invested. That, in turn, seemed like it could democratize access to the world's most sophisticated investing. I had no desire to be an entrepreneur, but I felt like I needed to pursue it for the social good.

I naively thought I would get the company going and then recruit a much more capable CEO with relevant experience within a year. Unfortunately, it took us three and a half years until we worked out all the kinks and launched our Robo advisor in December 2011, so I had to stay on as CEO much longer than I would have liked. We were not the first Robo advisor in the market, but we were the first one that offered our service at a fraction of what traditional advisors charged, so we were the first company in our space to take off and define the new category of Automated Investing (a . . . Robo advising). I'm proud to say that as of the completion of this book, we now have more than $50 billion under management and are still growing rapidly.

I was very excited when Elizabeth and Qian approached me to tell me about the book they were writing about Robo advising. The combination of their backgrounds makes them the ideal pair to write a book on the subject. Elizabeth is an international business journalist who served as Wealthfront's initial content editor. She played a huge role in defining the language that helped investors understand what a Robo advisor does and why it might make sense to use our service. One of our earliest engineers, Qian wrote the original code for several of the most important features of automated investing, including tax-loss harvesting. Tax-loss harvesting is arguably the greatest value of a Robo advisor, available to everyday investors for the first time. Elizabeth and Qian's deep knowledge and chemistry make this book an invaluable read if you care about growing your wealth.

They do a great job covering all the questions you might have before considering investing with a Robo advisor. First and foremost, they address the many misconceptions individual investors have around investing. You might be surprised to learn that nothing about good investing feels right, which is why so few people do it well. Once you understand the misconceptions, you'll understand how a Robo advisor can help you make money.

If you like to understand how something works before you buy it, you're in luck. Elizabeth and Qian explain in very simple language how Robo advisors deliver superior outcomes and how you can properly use them. They even provide the tools necessary to choose the right Robo advisor for you.

Before this book, determining which Robo advisor was appropriate for you was challenging. Many websites, blogs, and podcasts purport to help you solve this problem. But they can't be objective if they want to attract the advertisers they need to meet their financial goals. There is no right answer for everyone, but Elizabeth and Qian have made it easy to figure out which Robo advisor is right for you.

On a personal note, the friendships, professional connections, and even some marriages made over the years among Wealthfront employees mean a lot to me. It took outstanding groups of people years of hard work to make sophisticated, automated investment advice available to everyone. We built a company and launched a Robo advisor movement. The end of a book foreword is a rare moment in writing: an end, a beginning, and a handoff, all at once. Have fun reading this *Little Book*, as I did. You're in good hands: Elizabeth and Qian will show you how a Robo advisor builds an optimized portfolio for you so you can make money in your sleep.

Acknowledgments

———— ~ ————

THANKS TO OUR TEACHERS, reviewers, readers, and supporters, who are too many to list. Here are a few:

John Cummings, Marjorie Conner, Charley Ellis, Maggie Jing, Tao Jing, Christina Ku, Ying Liu, Burton Malkiel, Zara Stone, Jeff Rosenberger, Wei Wang, Athena Williams, and Janice and Omar.

Introduction

─────────────── ∽ ───────────────

BACK IN 2011, ELIZABETH was feeling decidedly disillusioned
with traditional Wall Street firms. As an editor for a business
newspaper in New York City, she had covered the 2008–09
financial crisis. Everyday investors, including Elizabeth, had
taken hits on their retirement savings while big companies
got bailouts. On a trip to California, she met Andy Rachleff
at a backyard party for investment advisors, where he was
gathering intel for the company he was launching.

He leaned awkwardly across a makeshift tiki bar to
look her in the eyes—he's six feet three, and she's a full foot
shorter. He explained himself and his idea in a voice so loud
someone could have heard it across the Grand Canyon.
People in Silicon Valley used to say, "No one says no to
Andy Rachleff." He eventually persuaded Elizabeth to join

Wealthfront, which in true lean start-up mode was operating out of a former dry cleaner's storefront in the center of Palo Alto. Andy was already a successful investor, but his big idea was to help regular people—anybody, in fact—invest well. He was putting together a team from outside the world of traditional finance, people who could think about the problems that investors faced with fresh eyes.

The company had many of the right pieces in place. Unlike brokerage firms, Wealthfront was registered as an investment advisor, for one thing. All online and offline registered financial advisors have a legal obligation to do what's in their clients' best interest, not theirs. The executive team was accomplished: Andy had cofounded one of the most successful investment companies of all time, a venture firm called Benchmark Capital. And as a trustee he helped oversee the endowment of the University of Pennsylvania. Eventually, famous economist and Princeton University Professor Burt Malkiel—a longtime advocate for individual investors—joined to design investment strategies. And so did a woman named Qian Liu, who was just coming out of the University of Pennsylvania and already building a reputation as one of the smartest people in financial technology, or fintech. Qian did groundbreaking technical work to build Wealthfront (and to invent the category of online investment advice), while Elizabeth established the language and narrative that helped launch the robo investment movement.

Wealthfront, as you probably know, took off, thanks to the whole team.

In 2023, Bill Falloon, a top editor at Wiley, asked Elizabeth about writing a robo investing book. Elizabeth in turn asked Qian to join the effort.

Both of us have known financial vulnerability. Elizabeth is a single mom with two kids, who worked her way through the University of Maryland with the help of scholarships and support from her family. Qian is an immigrant. In 2003, she arrived in the United States from China with a PhD scholarship to the University of Pennsylvania and $1,000 cash in her pocket, to rent a room in UPenn's graduate student dorm building. Qian's PhD advisor—then the department chair of the UPenn's computer science department and now an executive at Google—recommended her to Andy. At Wealthfront, she studied and passed the test to become a chartered financial analyst.

In other words, neither of us was an expert investor, and both of us, over time, learned how to use a robo investment platform with ease.. The two of us have stayed friends over the years. Qian and Elizabeth's kids have competed head-to-head in Taboo! Qian learned from them and almost won. Qian also learned how to outsmart dating apps' algorithms to actually meet decent people and shared that knowledge with Elizabeth. (If you make it to Chapter 9, you'll learn the secret and also how investing and dating are similar.)

Our Qualifications

Our own knowledge of investing comes from years of working in the finance and technology industries, helping everyday investors understand the market, economy, and technology.

In the years after Wealthfront, Qian went on to work for GoFundMe, an online social fundraising platform, and then as chief data officer for Guideline, an online investment platform that manages small business 401(k) plans. She's one of the hidden figures of the movement over the last 15 years to bring high-quality financial services to everyday investors.

After the Great Recession, Elizabeth traveled all over the world as a business journalist, writing about entrepreneurship in the Middle East, international trade, and always keeping an interest in personal finance and investing. She worked with the United Nations, Georgetown University, and Massachusetts Institute of Technology on projects to make the economic systems in the United States and abroad more fair for everyone. In 2021, she coauthored a book about how and why to invest in Main Street businesses, *The New Builders*.

We want to particularly express our appreciation for Burt Malkiel's A *Random Walk Down Wall Street*, Charley Ellis's *Winning the Loser's Game*, and David Swensen's *Unconventional Success*. In previous decades, these men were some of the first to advocate for a research-based approach to investing, one that puts the needs of everyday investors, not wealthy people, at heart. We love those books and are honored to have worked with Burt and Charley and to distill some of their wisdom into this *Little Book*.

The winter before Bill asked Elizabeth about writing the *Little Book of Robo Investing*, Qian and Elizabeth were in Costa Rica on a girls' trip: Qian was learning to surf. Elizabeth went on a yoga retreat. One lesson to be a successful investor is balance. And one gift of financial security is time: when you feel that you're set up for the long term, you can relax and splurge a little bit on the short term. Together, we wrote this book to teach you how to invest well, using a robo platform. By "invest well," we mean that you'll feel secure and confident about making enough money for your future so that you can relax and enjoy life more. Most investors spend way too much time and money trying to beat the market. Our approach is different: figure out how much money you need, and then invest as safely as possible to reach your goals. Robo investing was invented to help you do just that.

Let's put some numbers on our results on the platform. Since 2014, when she started using a robo investment platform, Elizabeth has almost doubled her retirement investment, earning a 90% return while taking a middling level of risk. Eventually, she started a taxable account because she knew the platform would help keep her taxes low; it has saved her about $1,100 in taxes in three years (from tax-loss harvesting, a feature introduced and popularized by Wealthfront, which will be explained at length in Chapter 6). Her cash, meanwhile, is returning 4.85% per year in the summer of 2023. These are good rates of return, and we'll tell you more about how the platform helped achieve them in the following chapters.

Qian started a Roth IRA and a taxable account at Wealthfront in December 2011 while developing the very first version of the company's investment software, as part of the "eating your own dog food" product development practice in the technology industry. She earned a higher return than Elizabeth did because she took more risk: so far the cumulative return in the two accounts are 120% and 140%, with estimated tax saving of about $5,200. Qian also used the company's line of credit feature, a button click triggering an instant cash transfer, and borrowed $10,000 at a low interest rate to pay an unexpected bill in early 2022, without having to sell her investments. She repaid the loan about 40 days later with $40 interest.

These are features pioneered by Wealthfront, which today is a thriving large company. Wealthfront was the first company to take off, but after we broke the ground, many other companies joined the industry. As of 2022 more than 7 million people use online investment advisors, or robo advisors or robo investing platforms (we use the terms interchangeably).[1] Like many good ideas, most of these features have spread across the industry. If you join the millions of investors using online services, these features will be available easily to you, too.

Both of us own Wealthfront stock, which is a significant asset for both of us but not the largest one we have. Our careers are more valuable than the stock. We're proud of what we helped build at Wealthfront, but we're prouder still of helping to invent this category—and to have companies from Vanguard, which now offers a robo advisor, to Robinhood follow in Wealthfront's path by offering financial services in mobile apps. There are a lot of options in the market today, and you need to be a smart shopper to decide what is best for you. We aim to be agnostic in this book. We'll give you the tools to evaluate robo investment platforms, to help decide which one is best for you. In Section 4, we offer a list of the major robo investment platforms in the market.

How the Book Works

We start each chapter with one misconception about investing and explain why it's harmful. Today's robo investment platforms have been designed to implement proven investing strategies. Those strategies are often counter to marketing from traditional financial services companies. We also want readers to understand why the platforms work the way they do so you can get the best out of them.

This book is divided into four sections. Section 1 defines investing today and offers a brief history of index investing and robo investing. Robo investing is a new way of investing, but it's built on a foundation of risk/reward theory, modern portfolio theory, and index investing. This foundation recognizes that most investors can't beat the market. Burt Malkiel is famous for saying, "You can't beat the market. So don't try. Focus on what you can control: diversification, fees, and taxes." You'll do better than most investors, and you'll have a great chance of making money over time.

Section 2 is about the pillars of robo investing platforms and how to maximize your after-tax returns. Section 3 contains insights from behavioral finance that will help you set financial goals and overcome the basic human tendency to be too focused on the short term. Sections 2 and 3, combined, will help you come up with a plan, stick to it when you should, and shift when it's time. And Section 4 is about how to get started. The most important thing to us is that after you've finished reading this short book, you'll feel confident enough to start. You can't change the past, but the future is yours.

Section One

---~---

The Science,
Business, and Art
of Robo Investing

---~---

Chapter One

Make Investing Work for You

———— ❧ ————

A FEW YEARS AGO, A friend of Elizabeth's, Jodi, reached out for advice about what to do with a bonus check of $20,000.* She already had an employer-managed retirement plan at work, but she didn't pay much attention to it. And now with a small windfall, she had the vague idea that she should invest. She looked up Apple's stock price and wondered whether Elizabeth thought this was a good stock to buy.

---

*Jodi's name has been changed.

And maybe a few others, such as Lululemon, and some shares of Tesla?

"Where to begin?" Elizabeth asked herself. Jodi was falling foul of one of the biggest misconceptions about investing, the first of many misconceptions we're going to debunk in this book.

Jodi's question, and dozens of others over the years from our family and friends, helped us decide to write this book. Investing isn't taught in school, and over the years, lots of smart and well-educated people have asked us questions that tell us they have been misinformed about investing. They don't realize there is a research-based approach to investing, one with an unexpected key: relax! In fact, making money in the markets today is so easy that you can make money in your sleep. Some people maximize effort to get rich, and they usually fail. We want to minimize stress. And when you do that, you'll be surprised at how well you do financially.

We've written this book for people who are interested in joining a robo investment platform and those who are already on robo investment platforms but are not using them as well or easily as they might. Robo investing is great for people who have as little as $50 a month to invest, because you can quickly establish and adjust an emergency savings account earning some of the highest interest rates around. If you're in your 20s, we say: run, don't walk, to set up a low-cost retirement account on a robo platform that will make money for you in your sleep; do not fall for financial services industry marketing that implies you'll succeed trading individual stocks or trying to beat the market! For more on this, see Chapter 3. Robo investing is perfect for millionaire (or soon-to-be millionaire) cheapskates: people who want the high quality of traditional investment advice without paperwork hassles, high cost or high account minimum.

To learn the robo investing approach, you need to follow along in this short book. You'll need to unlearn some of what you know. Because there's so little accurate information about investing, many people operate under misconceptions about what works, what doesn't, and what works best.

Robo platforms apply the understanding developed in the last century about the nature of people and the nature of markets to become—on your behalf—the most disciplined investors. They'll help you meet your goals, taking the level of risk you decide you're comfortable with. Robo investment platforms also put many of the best tools that weren't accessible to everyday investors before, such as tax-loss harvesting and financial planning tools, in reach of everyone by moving them online. The combination of the research-based approach to investing and the easy-to-use tools is like a fine-tuned investment engine. You point it in the right direction and decide how fast you want to go—and then, you can relax.

We believe it's important to understand the concepts of investing and the innards of how robo investment platforms work to employ them. That way, you won't panic or take too much risk or be distracted by the "best new DIY investment idea" you hear about at your neighborhood barbeque or via your news app. Emotions have a way of getting the best of all of us, especially when it comes to the excitement of a get-rich-quick scheme. Luckily, robo investment platforms offer a lot of support for the rational side of our brains.

There is a *slightly* hard part about robo investing. You need to understand yourself, your goals, your needs, and your relationship with money, to tell the robo investment platform what it needs to know to design a portfolio for you and to stick with your plan. This little book will also go over some of the common emotional pitfalls that humans encounter around questions of money.

After you read this book, you'll know how to meet your long-term goals, including retirement and helping your family. You'll know how to invest for medium-term goals, such as big vacations, sabbaticals, and work on your home. Maybe you'll be like the investor who told the *Wall Street Journal* that using a robo investment platform was his version of TikTok! True story![1] It is fun to invest well, not because you're trading individual stocks, but because you wake up every morning feeling that you're on track financially in each phase of your life.

Knowing How to Use a Robo Platform Is a Superpower

A couple of quick asides before we start with the first misconception many Americans—including Jodi—have about investing.

First of all, you're ahead of the game if you're here. Only about 70% of working Americans invest at all, even for retirement, and those are mostly through workplace retirement plans.[2] You know as well as we do the pressures and rewards of today's economy. It's important for you to invest because stocks and bonds have historically delivered high enough returns to beat inflation.

It's unlikely that you can retire securely without investing, and investing is one of the few actions (in addition to buying a home, starting a business, or getting an education) that can help you build wealth. Over the past half century, from 1973 to 2022, the US stock market has returned an average of 11.7% per year.[3] If you had put $1 in the market in 1973 and left it there, untouched, you would have $253 today. If you had put $10,000 in, you would have more than $2.5 million today! With a more moderate assumption of 7 percent annual return, a $10,000 investment today would grow to $76,000 in 30 years, and $294,000 in 50 years. A quick-and-easy rule derived from the 7% annual return assumption is that your money in the market will roughly double every 10 years.[†] This is the reason you should invest: so that you, too, can take advantage of the market's magic[‡] to double your money every 10 years.

One image to capture the upward movement of the stock market over time is the idea of you, the investor, walking up a hill, while you are yo-yo-ing.[§] Your portfolio—the yo-yo—may go up and down, but if you keep walking, the portfolio will climb, too. You need to pick up the yo-yo and start walking. There are no absolute guarantees in life, but investing broadly in the market is one of the best financial bets there is.

You're also ahead of the game because you're considering robo investing platforms in your toolbox. Robo investing is

---

[†]Going forward it is more realistic to expect the US stock market to return on average 7% per year, rather than 11.7%. We will use 7% as the long-term average annual return assumption for the US stock market in the book.

[‡]It's not actually magic, of course, but mathematics, which seems incomprehensible to most of us. The human mind is stuck in a short-term survival mode, not built to see the long-term power of compounding.

[§]We heard first this image shared on a radio show hosted by financial advisor Ric Edelman.

the biggest innovation in the investment space in the past several decades; the platforms give you access to tools previously reserved for wealthy investors. And robo investing platforms are as safe as, or safer than, other kinds of financial firms. Robo investment platforms are regulated by the Securities and Exchange Commission (SEC) as fiduciaries, which means they are required by law to act in your best interest. Your investment accounts on robo investment platforms are insured up to $500,000 by the federal government to protect you against the firm's insolvency, as accounts would be with a traditional bank or advisory service. Cash deposits on robo investment platforms are often insured at multiples of $250,000, higher than some traditional banks. The federal government issues insurance to ensure the stability of the US financial system; robo investment platforms are part of the regulated system.

It's easy to set up an account on a robo investment platform; you can usually do that within five minutes. Most people start investing by connecting a bank account to a robo investment platform and transferring money. Connecting to your bank account is automatic and instant, with the transfer of funds taking a few days or instant at the most advanced platforms. Robo investment platforms have some of the easiest websites and mobile apps to use. We'll get into all of this in more detail later, but we wanted you to feel grounded before we hit the investing concepts.

What Is Investing Today?

Now, let's go! Back to Elizabeth's friend Jodi and the misconception she was laboring under when she asked for advice. She was thinking that she might buy Apple and Tesla. They might be great companies, but Jodi was falling prey to the first misconception about investing.

Misconception #1: Investing means buying individual stocks.

If you believe this and buy individual stocks, you will be putting yourself at unnecessary financial risk and probably pay too much in fees and taxes, to boot. Investing does not mean buying individual stocks. Here's a simple-and-true definition of investing, a foundation to build on:

Investing is the art of driving an increase in your net worth over the long term, meaning more than three years.

In the past, people thought buying individual stocks (and bonds), or keeping money in interest-producing cash products, was the best way to increase their net worth over time. But research in recent decades has definitively established that people are terrible at consistently picking winning stocks, so terrible that picking winning stocks is nearly impossible.

Picking stocks has also gotten harder. In today's information-saturated environment, markets work incredibly efficiently to establish prices. That means the price you pay for a stock (or a bond) is very likely to be the price anyone else would pay, which means it's almost impossible to consistently buy stocks at a discount and sell them at a premium.

If you could predict the future about an individual stock, of course, you could overcome the problem of information saturation: you'd know something that the person trading across from you wouldn't know about the stock. But you don't—the person trading across from you knows as much as you do, and you do not have an edge over them.

Robo investment platforms use a particular tool, index funds, to invest for you. Optimized combinations of index funds representing different asset classes help you make money and manage the inevitable risk of investing. We're going to explain index funds and asset classes next and return to them in more detail later in the book.

What Is an Index Fund?

Here's what Elizabeth said to Jodi, roughly: people used to trade more in individual stocks and bonds, and in fact tried to invest for their futures that way. But stocks and bonds bought one at a time or in small handfuls are extremely risky. What if you were holding a lot of AT&T stock when the news broke that the company might be responsible for miles of decade-old lead-covered telecom? That dividend-producing stock *looked* safe. But no individual stock is very safe. Consider Carnival Cruise lines. In December 2019, the stock looked like smooth sailing ahead, based on the population of cruise-loving baby boomers. In December 2019, Carnival's stock was trading at $45. By April 1, 2020, after the start of a global pandemic, whose exact timing nobody could have predicted, the stock was down to $11. Even if you are the rare person able and lucky enough to pick a big winner or two, you'll erase your gains with other bad bets or mistakes in timing. The fact of owning individual stocks means you're more likely to trade them (because that's what you think you ought to do). Owning individual stocks is detrimental to investors' long-term returns because investors tend to buy and sell them more often. Even when they try to invest in many stocks at once, everyday investors invariably get the timing wrong because they are human. They sell in a panic or buy with overconfidence.

Index funds make investing cheaper and less risky by allowing investors to hold shares of many stocks representing a broad market at once and by encouraging investors to buy and hold. They were invented in the middle of the 20th century, based on the idea that while nobody can accurately predict the ups and downs of single stocks over the long term, we can reasonably bet that the entire economy, represented by the stock market, will grow. One example of an index fund is an S&P 500 index fund that mirrors the combined, weighted stock performances of the largest 500 companies trading in the US stock market. Another is a Wilshire 5000 index fund, which mirrors the performance of 5,000 stocks of US public companies, small, medium, and large. Today, about 68,000 companies around the world have issued shares that trade on public markets, in countries from the United States to France to Brazil. In the United States, where the markets are the biggest, about 6,000 company stocks trade publicly.[4]

A relatively new format of index funds trade on the market, called Exchanged-Traded Funds (ETFs). As of this writing in August 2023, the price for a share of Vanguard's Total Stock Market ETF was $221, up from $149 five years ago. When you buy an index fund, you bet that a very large swath of the market (the swath mirrored by the index fund) will go up over time. If you buy an S&P 500 index fund, you're betting that the 500 largest companies in the United States will grow, even if they aren't the same 500 companies over time. If you buy an index fund that mirrors the bond market, you're betting most of the companies and governments will make good on their promises to pay bondholders. That means that you, the individual investor, can capture the returns (and risk) of that part of the market.

The Key Concept of Asset Classes

From the beginning of the public markets, stocks (and different kinds of stocks), bonds, and cash have always behaved differently: stocks move up and down in price more often, and over the long term, go up the most as an asset class. Bonds are less volatile. It's easier to predict their prices because there is income attached to them. And cash, of course, becomes more or less appealing as an investment as interest rates rise and fall.

As computers advanced in the late 20th century, it began to be possible to create new combinations of stocks, bonds, real estate, and cash vehicles to create well-defined categories. In the language of investing, stocks, bonds, real estate, and cash are assets. They're grouped into categories called asset classes. Thanks to investment research starting in the 1950s, it is possible to make pretty good predictions of how asset classes will behave over the long term and to create combinations of them that give you the best statistical chance to grow your portfolio with the least amount of risk. This is somewhat analogous to our advances in predicting the weather accurately. Weather forecasters can't predict with perfect specificity and accuracy. But they can tell you how different variables act on each other to create different kinds of weather and make broad predictions based on that information.

We're actually a little better at predicting asset classes' long-term returns than the weather, possibly because human-created systems, while complicated, are less complicated than short-term weather systems. We can predict how asset classes are likely to rise and fall over time in different environments. And research also established that the most profitable way to invest in asset classes is index funds.

You Can Use Index Funds to Invest in Many Different Kinds of Asset Classes

Robo investment platforms use index funds representing asset classes including US stocks, international stocks, bonds, and real estate (and others—we'll talk more about this in Chapter 4). Each of these asset classes has an expected return. It's reasonable, based on a very long history, to expect US stocks to return 7% a year. It's reasonable to expect US bonds to return 4–5% a year. Cash, which is another kind of asset class, is returning upwards of 4% a year as of 2023 summer because the Federal Reserve has been raising interest rates, but that high return looks unlikely to last for more than a year or two.

Index funds make investing a lot simpler than buying individual stocks and bonds. How can anyone know whether a big chip maker such as Nvidia (currently one of the five most valuable stocks in the US) is going to be allowed to sell chips in China? If it can, it'll grow faster and its stock has a better chance of rising. Meanwhile, if the US government says no, the stock could drop. You'd have to be inside the heads of US and Chinese government officials, Nvidia executives and lobbyists, and you'd have to figure out whether . . . oh . . . there might be a global event that is going to cause the whole market to crater!

So Here Is Our Practical Definition of Robo Investing

Robo investing is a research-based, low-cost, automated method of driving a reasonably predictable increase in your net worth over the long term by using portfolios of index funds representing different asset classes.

Robo investment platforms do the complicated work of combining index funds, representing the asset classes, incredibly well. In the process, they have a secret weapon to increase your after-tax profits: tax-loss harvesting, which we'll get to in Chapter 6.

Stock-Picking Is Boring and Painful When You're Not Making Money

Some people get paid good money to make educated guesses about events such as the above example of Nvidia, and even those professionals' guesses mostly turn out to be wrong. But for most people, even attempting to do this kind of investment work is *boring*. Once you realize you're not likely to get rich, what's the point? If you wanted to keep track of the earning potential of thousands of companies in the markets or evaluate the risk of the next big catastrophic event such as a pandemic, you would have become a Wall Street professional or an economist, which you did not, because you're reading our book. Index funds work a lot better for individual investors. If you buy an index fund, you're buying the returns of the market, for a tiny fee (it doesn't cost much to create and run an index fund).

Investing with index funds means you're lessening the risk of owning individual stocks, but it's important to note you're also buying the risk of particular swaths of the market, which can go down, too. There are ways to minimize your risk—by buying index funds representing different swaths, or asset classes, and holding your investments over a long time. A robo investment platform will help you do both. But it's important to note that even with good index funds that you buy through a robo investment platform, you can't escape some risk. Investing is about taking some risks to be rewarded with returns. Everything in life has a price. There is a night and a day, a yin and yang, a risk and a reward. The keys to managing investment risk are time and diversification, as we'll talk about in Chapters 3 and 4.

Shortcut to Robo Investing

If you're the kind of person who learns by doing, you can go ahead and skip to the last section of the book, Section 4, which is about how to get started on a robo investment platform. It's really easy: you can set up an account in a matter of minutes, move a little money into it, and start experimenting. As of summer 2023, there were 13 widely recognized robo investment platforms in the market. Section 4 will also offer some information about how you should pick one.

But we'd like you to read Sections 1–3 because we believe you'll be better equipped to set your financial goals and to use the robo investment platforms to their fullest extent. And you'll be more likely to stick to your investing plans when the market takes a dive, as it inevitably will.

The Nobel Prize–winning economists who created the theoretical foundation of robo investing were, respectively, Paul Samuelson, Eugene Fama, Harry Markowitz, and Daniel Kahneman; and more economists and industry practitioners contributed empirical evidence supporting the low-cost, broadly diversified and behavioral approach to investing. We go into their research in more detail in Sections 2–3. Using software invented early in the 21st century, robo investment platforms turned the discoveries of these researchers into innovations for everyday investors. Robo investment platforms use risk questionnaires to consider your age, your finances, and your goals. Then they assess different index funds for their fees and qualities and construct a broadly diversified portfolio for you. They also respond to changes in the market, keeping your portfolio balanced and minimizing your taxes (in your taxable accounts, if you have them).

Final Note

Investing with index funds on robo investment platforms is not a get-rich-quick scheme. They're about doing well as an investor while exerting as little effort as possible. With a nod to Megan Trainor: *if beating the market is what you're into, then go ahead and move along.* This may not be the book for you (though you are welcome to stick around for a challenge, and we hope you do). In this book, you'll learn that the idea of beating the market is a mirage.** Investing well and meeting your financial goals so you can spend time on your career, your hobbies, and your passions can be a reality.

**The beat-the-market mirage propagated by the investment industry is like Barbie's physical proportions: a completely unrealistic idea that is so appealing that it became the unattainable standard. Mattel reduced the doll's bust size in 1998 and introduced differently shaped dolls over the years. Even so, a real-life woman with the physique of stereotypical Barbie would not be able to walk because of her overly large head and long, thin curves.

Key Takeaways in This Chapter

1. Investing is not buying individual stocks. Investing is driving an increase in your net worth over more than three years.

2. Asset classes are categories of return-producing property that you own, such as stocks, bonds, real estate, and cash (that's earning interest). Nobel Prize–winning research in the 20th century and empirical studies enabled people to predict how different asset classes behave over the long term.

3. Asset classes have different risk/reward profiles. Stocks are the riskiest and have the highest rates of return. Other kinds of asset classes enable you to reduce the risk of owning stocks, while still earning an impressive return.

4. The ideal way to invest in different asset classes is through index funds, which make investing cheaper and safer, so you can earn the market's returns, which have been very good over time. But you also take on the risk of the market, which goes down periodically.

5. Index funds and robo investing are innovations based on research.

6. Robo investing is a research-based, low-cost, automated method of driving a reasonably predictable increase in your net worth over the long term by using portfolios of index funds representing different asset classes.

Language of Investing[††]

Assets: property.

Asset classes: categories of income-producing property that you can invest in.

Speculating: buy property, such as gold or cryptocurrency, or assume a business risk hoping to make a large short-term profit from market fluctuations. Speculative investments often produce no income, which means their prices are more subject to fluctuation.

Stock: an ownership share in a company that technically gives you a claim to the future income produced by the company.

Bond: a slice of debt issued by a company, government, or a nonprofit entity that promises interest payments.

Index fund: the ideal way to invest in asset classes because they're cheaper and less risky.

Portfolio: your collection of assets and asset classes.

Return: profit.

(*Continued*)

[††]It's not clear why the investment world has a different language. Often, language is used to exclude people. We suspect this is the case when it comes to the processes and information necessary to build wealth, or "capital."

After-tax return: profit after the investment taxes (see Chapter 6).

Risk: price fluctuation, volatility.

The S&P 500 index: A hypothetical portfolio consisting of the largest 500 stocks in the US public stock market, as a representation of the market. S&P stands for Standard & Poor's, the former name of the company who owns and maintains the index (now called S&P Global Ratings).

History of Stocks and Bonds

The first stock was sold by The Dutch East India Co. on the Amsterdam Stock Exchange in the early 1600s to fund voyages. Investors were willing to bankroll expensive voyages in exchange for a slice of the potential profit from the spice trade. The investment was speculative—it could be fantastically lucrative if a voyage was successful, or it could evaporate if the ship sank in the Atlantic Ocean. The capital raised allowed The Dutch East India Co. to set more sails and expand its business. It was once worth almost $8 trillion in today's dollars, even more valuable than Apple, the most valuable company right now and worth $2.82 trillion.

Companies sell stocks to investors to raise capital to operate their businesses. When you buy a share of a company's stock, either from the company directly or another investor, you own a slice of the company. As a shareholder, you are entitled to the company's future profit proportional to your slice. Amazon's stock price grew eight-fold in the last 10 years. If you had bought Amazon's shares for $1,000 10 years ago, they would be worth $8,000 today, a phenomenal return delivered by Amazon to its investors.

Bonds are much older than stocks. The first bond was a government bond issued by the city-state of Venice to fund its war against Constantinople in the 1100s. Venetian citizens bought the bond (i.e., lent money to Venice's government) and got paid a 5% interest rate.

Today, a bond is a slice of debt issued by a company, government, or a nonprofit entity that promises interest payments and repayment of the principal. The bond evolved over time to incorporate features such as semiannual interest payments. Modern bonds, like stocks, can be traded on the market.

Bonds last for a certain amount of time, usually six months to 30 years and in rare occasions as long as 100 years.[‡‡] After you buy a bond you can either hold the

(*Continued*)

[‡‡]We had the same question: Why would someone buy a 100-year bond, if they're never going to get the money? Apparently, institutions buy them.

bond and accept the interest, or sell the bond to someone else who wants the future interest payments and is willing to pay a price for that income. Bond prices are set by a few factors: the interest paid by the issuing entity to the holder of the bond, the creditworthiness of the issuing entity (or government entity), time to maturity, and the prevailing interest rates at the time. Bond prices fluctuate as each of the factors evolve. Bond prices can be volatile, too, such as when inflation suddenly spiked in 2022, which caused a large increase in interest rates and drop in bond prices.

Chapter Two

A Brief History of Indexing and Robo Investing

HAVE YOU HEARD OF a concierge doctor? Most doctors are paid by insurance companies depending on how many tests and procedures they perform. But concierge doctors don't accept insurance. Instead, you pay them a flat fee each year to be on call for you, to treat you for basic medical problems and to help you find specialists if you need them. Concierge doctors got started in part because doctors hate the paperwork of insurance companies almost as much (maybe more) than patients do. They're growing more popular because they work well: Their financial incentives are aligned with their patients' care. If they keep you healthy, you won't call as often. They also don't have a financial incentive to order unnecessary tests for you, because they won't be paid any more or less for sending you for extra scans.

In the business world, this is known as aligning incentives. In the investment industry, there are some companies whose incentives are aligned with yours and some whose incentives are not aligned with yours.

Misconception #2: If you use an investment company, it's working for you.

Robo investment platforms work well in part because their incentives are aligned with yours. But there are a lot of other investment companies, including some new online companies, whose business models work differently. In this chapter, we're going to give you a fast history of the investment industry so that you can better recognize which companies are more apt to work for you. It's hard for companies to change their underlying business models, so once you understand how a company makes money, you can be reasonably sure it won't change over time. By the way, we know this chapter won't be for everyone! And if you want to skip ahead to other more practical parts of the book, you can put this chapter in the back of your mind, for when you see a news headline that makes you uneasy about whether your money is safe with whatever company you have picked.

Public Stock Trading

Public stock trading in America got started about 125 years ago in New York City. Public stock trading meant anyone with money could buy a share in a company. Companies that are publicly held are required to be transparent about their operations and prospects.[*]

Back in the late 1800s, your portfolio might have included stock in US Steel and General Motors and bonds issued by General Electric. But this was hard and a little bit risky. How could you possibly know enough about the steel industry, electricity, and cars all at once, not to mention about the global economy, to know whether these companies would do well in their respective markets. And what if a calamity befell all three companies at once? The investors of a century ago were well aware of global catastrophes: they had just emerged from World War I and from the influenza pandemic of 1918–1920.

---

[*] Private investing exists, too; in fact, many fast-growing companies that eventually become public get off the ground with investments by private investors, who are typically wealthier.

In 1924, some bright minds at the MIE Massachusetts Investors' Trust in Boston established the first modern mutual fund to manage the risks of trading in individual stocks. A mutual fund holds a basket of stocks, sometimes many stocks and sometimes a handful. Mutual funds were invented to help people reduce the risk (and hassle) of investing in one company at a time. A calamity might befall General Electric, but the chances a calamity would befall General Electric, US Steel, and General Motors at once were somewhat lower. Investors quickly realized mutual funds were a good idea, and the number of them grew.

The concept was adapted to real estate companies so investors could hold shares in companies that operate buildings and to bonds so that investors could hold many bonds at once through a mutual fund. Mutual fund companies put a lot of work into designing and running funds that focus on different industries and that make different kinds of bets on the direction of the economy. The fund companies then sell shares in their mutual funds to the public. You'll be familiar with some of the names of today's big mutual fund companies, such as Fidelity and T. Rowe Price. You also hear them called asset managers.

The Index Revolution

By the 1970s, the markets were humming along. American capitalism was doing its work; investors were buying and selling stocks, bonds, and real estate, in many cases through mutual funds. But there was a problem: mutual funds were expensive to operate, and their returns sometimes were not high enough to justify the fees. Inspired by a new theory called efficient market hypothesis and empirical studies of mutual fund performance, some revolutionaries began to guess that there might be a better way to invest than mutual fund managers' stock picking.

Among the revolutionaries were economists Burt Malkiel and Charley Ellis (who both advised Wealthfront). These economists observed that, over time, no mutual funds or smart investors can consistently beat the market. Part of the problem was how complicated the global economy was becoming, and another part was how much the professional investors were charging. The cost incurred by mutual funds was a major contributor to their underperformance compared to the market.

These economists suggested creating a new kind of mutual fund, an index fund, that mirrored the market instead of trying to beat it. In 1974, a disillusioned mutual fund company CEO, Jack Bogle, founded a company, Vanguard. It went on to produce most of the first index funds for individual investors. Today, Vanguard remains the lowest-cost provider of funds because of its big emphasis on indexing. Though it does offer actively managed mutual funds, it has a unique nonprofit corporate structure that means it has an incentive to keep the prices on all its funds, index funds, and mutual funds low.[†]

The evidence rolled in swiftly. Mutual fund investing and stock picking—also called active management—kept underperforming the market net of fees, while index investors were matching it. Burt Malkiel called this the index advantage. You can see one example of how mutual funds underperform one index, the S&P 500, in the following chart.[1] For the 20-year time period ending 2022, the S&P 500 returned 9.8% per year. The average US equity fund returned 8.92% per year, and the average US large-cap equity fund returned 8.16% per year, substantially underperforming the S&P 500 by 0.88% and 1.64% per year, respectively.

In index funds, no research is required to pick stocks that might outperform the market. Since research is the biggest cost of operating a mutual fund, the savings from no research are passed along to investors in the form of lower management fees. Index investing was cheaper, easier, and simpler. And it was working. By the end of the Great Recession, in 2010, index funds were entrenched, accounting for about 19% of the total fund market. (In 2022, they were 50%.[2]) Many of the big mutual fund companies began offering index funds, too. But they were making more money from

---

[†] The company had $7.6 trillion of assets under management (AUM) as of March 2023.

Average U.S. Equity Fund Performance Ending 2022 (Equal-Weighted)

Category	3-Year (Annualized, %)	5-Year (Annualized, %)	10-Year (Annualized, %)	20-Year (Annualized, %)
S&P Composite 1500	7.59	9.15	12.40	9.92
All Domestic Funds	5.32	6.43	10.83	8.92
S&P 500	7.66	9.42	12.56	9.80
All Large-Cap Funds	5.81	7.27	10.25	8.16

Source: Adapted from SPIVA U.S. Scorecard 2023.

the old-style mutual funds. As you can see from these stats, people were still buying and selling actively managed funds. There were a few good reasons for that. Some higher-priced mutual funds are good for particular investment purposes. Institutions can own shares in a part of the market that doesn't have a great index, for instance. But another reason mutual funds remain popular is that they are more profitable for the mutual fund companies. To sell them, companies who created the actively managed mutual funds have a sales force: stockbrokers. They pay some stockbrokers, whose job it is to place trades, healthy commissions to sell particularly expensive mutual funds. This is akin to the medical device companies who give doctors a kickback for referring patients to their facilities. You're paying more and potentially getting a scan you don't need.

What to Do about Conflicts of Interest?

Partly in response to the conflicts of interest, knowledgeable investors (usually the wealthy ones) hired registered investment advisors instead of stockbrokers to help them manage their investments. Registered investment advisors also help investors buy and sell investments, but they are regulated differently, by the Securities and Exchange Commission. They agree to abide by the fiduciary standard. The standard imposes upon the advisor the "affirmative duty of 'utmost good faith' and full and fair disclosure of material facts" as part of the advisor's duty to exercise loyalty and care. This includes "an obligation not to subordinate the clients' interests to its own."

Brokerages, the companies stockbrokers work for, don't have to abide by the fiduciary standard. They're regulated by the Financial Industry Regulatory Authority. Companies such as Merrill Lynch, Charles Schwab, and TD Ameritrade, or people working for them, can sell you a high-priced mutual fund without telling you that they have a conflict of interest: A commission from the company. In the past, they also charged a lot to place trades, and therefore, had an interest in encouraging you to trade. This is less the case today because of the adoption of commission-free trading promoted by Robinhood, but Robinhood's interest isn't aligned with investors' either—more on this later in the book.

This world isn't black-and-white. There are good, ethical stockbrokers and registered investment advisors who are rotten apples.[‡] But the regulation and the legal structure give investors who use registered investment advisors an extra layer of protection.

Many registered investment advisors put their clients into better-quality, less expensive funds, mostly index funds, because they don't have an incentive to do otherwise. They also offer important tools that make it easier to invest and that improve after-tax returns. Because registered investment advisors are paid on a fee basis depending on the amount of assets you have—akin to the concierge doctors—they typically require high account minimums. Many registered investment advisors have minimums that start at $500,000, charging 1% a year (that's $5,000!). To justify the high fees and build their clients' portfolios, registered investment advisors offer all kinds of tools, including one that robo investment platforms were able to move online, called tax-loss harvesting, which we'll talk about in detail in Chapter 6. Only the wealthy could afford to pay high-priced advisors for the personalized investment decisions that take into account which investments are high quality, what age you are and, therefore, what your risk level should be, and how to minimize tax bills.

[‡] As a famous example, Bernie Madoff lied to his clients.

By the late 20th century, individual investors had lots of choices about whether to invest in individual stocks and bonds (not a good idea, too risky) or in a variety of different funds, including index funds and heavily marketed mutual funds. But how to pick, and when to buy and sell? If you couldn't afford to pay for a registered investment advisor and you wanted to invest in addition to your workplace retirement plan, you were out swimming alone, likely clinging to a confusing brochure from your company's human resources office,[§] or relying on an expensive and (maybe) ethical stockbroker for help. That's when, around 2010, the robo investment platforms entered the scene.

Part Two of the Index Revolution

Robo investment platforms started appearing around 2008–09. They adopted the ethics and regulatory structure of the registered investment advisors and the sensibilities of the index revolutionaries: Don't try to beat the market, and invest for the long term (we'll talk more about why they did that in the next chapter). They designed their platforms to support investors in those behaviors.

[§] Confronted with these brochures, people tend to confuse the investment they're looking at with the company offering it. They'll say, "My Fidelity" is doing well—when what's really doing well is the particular fund offered by Fidelity.

They were able to push the index revolution a little bit further, however, because they came along as a result of a handful of technological and financial advances. The mutual fund industry began offering index funds in the form of exchange-traded funds (ETFs) in 1993. Because ETFs are funds that trade as easily as individual stocks, the universe of possible investments expanded, giving the new software-based platforms more combinations of stocks, bonds, and other assets to work with. Application programming interfaces (APIs) modernized the plumbing of the financial system. APIs enabled the platforms to trade ETFs electronically without human brokers in the loop. The elimination of human brokers led to a much lower cost to operate a robo investing business, which was passed along in the form of lower platform fees to customers. APIs, which connected bank accounts, provided stock price feeds, and verified customer identity, were integrated with robo platforms' website and smartphone apps and made their customer experience seamless. The development of ETFs and APIs also enabled robo platforms to provide their products at a much lower account minimum of hundreds of dollars and open access to regular individual investors.

People had tried versions of automated financial advice before. In the early 2010s, people were ready to listen. After the 2008 financial crisis, many people lost trust in the investment professionals working on Wall Street. That gave the newcomers an opening. Millennials, the biggest generation by population, were in their 20s and 30s and comfortable with technology. Many earned stable income from work but still couldn't afford the account minimum, typically $100,000+, required by traditional human financial advisors. The phone-based communication perfected by their mom and dad's human investment advisors felt antiquated and unfit for their app-savvy lifestyle.

Wealthfront and Betterment were the first online financial advisors, also called robo financial advisors or robo investment platforms. Within a few years, many of the big fund companies, including Vanguard and Fidelity, had launched their own versions of online financial advisors. These companies charge a fee for their services based on the amount of money they manage for you. Like the concierge doctors we talked about at the beginning of the chapter, their incentives are aligned with yours: When your accounts do well, they get paid more.

Robo Investment Platforms versus Online Brokerages

The robo investment platforms (we list them in Chapter 14) have one important thing in common with traditional financial advisors: They are regulated by the Securities and Exchange Commission as fiduciaries. That means they have to, by law, abide by the fiduciary standard, which requires them to put clients' interests first.

Online brokerage started with ETrade (now part of Morgan Stanley) in 1992. After the first robo investment platforms moved financial advice online, more and different brokerage services appeared online. And because the brokerages were regulated at a lower level, they were free to design business models that didn't always put the customer first. The most famous recent example of a mobile-app brokerage is Robinhood, which turned stock trading into what seemed like a game during the pandemic. The mobile-app brokerage was different from its older counterparts in one way. It didn't charge commissions on trading or on high-priced mutual funds. But it did encourage people to trade individual stocks. Trading in individual stocks is risky for all the reasons we detailed in Chapter 1.

Robinhood also encouraged people to trade in options. Options are magnified bets on stock price: investors can purchase options that give them the right to buy shares at one price even if the market has priced them at another. You might pay $10 each for 10 call options, which costs you a total of $100 cash, for the right (but not the obligation) to buy shares of AT&T at a strike price of $100 per share. If the share price goes up to $120, you would exercise the options and end up with $200 (= $20 share price increase times 10 shares). After you subtract the amount you paid for the options ($100), you have a profit of $100; this is significantly more than a profit of $20 you'd make by simply buying one share with the $100 cash. If the share price decreases, unfortunately, to $99, the options would expire worthless and you would lose the $100 you paid for the options; this is also significantly more than a loss of $1 you'd suffer by buying one share with the $100 cash. Share prices go up and down all the time. Options magnify your losses when share prices move against you.

Robinhood (and other brokerages) have business models that depend on how much trading their customers do. Although users don't pay Robinhood for trading commissions, Robinhood bundled and sold their trading orders to larger companies on Wall Street to make money. Here's how the company was described by *Forbes* journalists Jeff Kauflin and Antoine Gara.

From its inception, Robinhood was designed to profit by selling its customers' trading data to the very sharks on Wall Street who have spent decades—and made billions—outmaneuvering investors. In fact, an analysis reveals that the more risk Robinhood's customers take in their hyperactive trading accounts, the more the Silicon Valley startup profits from the whales it sells their orders to. And while Robinhood's successful recruitment of inexperienced young traders may have inadvertently minted a few new millionaires riding the debt-fueled bull market, it is also deluding an entire generation into believing that trading options successfully is as easy as leveling up on a video game.[3]

In the famous case of GameStop, which happened in February 2021, small investors used options trading to counter moves by Wall Street hedge funds that were driving down the stock of a brick-and-mortar video game seller. Briefly, they seemed to win. But most eventually lost as Robinhood—which owed its allegiance to the companies that it was selling trading data to—stopped trading on its platform in response to the frenzy.

You can make the case that Robinhood turned many young people into traders, which arguably could be a gateway to becoming real investors. And when it offered free trading, it forever changed the brokerage industry, and many of the other brokerages followed suit. It's hard not to root for the little guy going up against the hedge funds on Wall Street and winning. But the reality of Robinhood and other online brokerages that sprang up in the wake of its success is a lot more complicated. Online brokerages hooked a lot of young people on the junk food of the investing world, trading.

In 2020 the Securities and Exchange Commission charged Robinhood with misleading customers, and the company agreed to pay $65 million to settle.[4] In 2021 the

Financial Industry Regulatory Authority (FINRA) fined Robinhood $70 million,[5] the largest fine in the agency's history, for misleading customers. In 2022 Robinhood's crypto arm was fined $30 million by New York State's financial regulator.[6] The company has cleaned up its act some since then. But company culture is hard to change, which is why we regard Robinhood and online brokerages in general with a lot of wariness. The brokerages, both the traditional ones and the new online versions, have succeeded in part because of a prevailing misconception that we're going to take on in the next chapter: the idea that you, an individual investor, can beat the market.

Key Takeaways in This Chapter

1. Not all investment companies work for you.
2. Some companies and individuals make money as your portfolio grows. Some make money when you trade. Over the long term, you're better off when their incentives are aligned with yours, as in the first case.
3. Registered investment advisors have a fiduciary duty to put their clients' interests first. Stockbrokers do not.
4. Robo investment platforms are registered investment advisors that operate online. They make money mostly from fees proportional to the assets they manage for you.
5. Brokers have increasingly moved online, too, but they make money when investors trade.

Asset Classes Index Funds Can Hold

Most robo investment platforms use an exchange-traded version of index funds, exchange-traded funds (ETFs), which are traded throughout the day. Index funds hold all kinds of different assets, including stocks, bonds, and real estate, and different kinds of each. For instance, you could buy an index fund that mirrors the performance of a group of dividend-producing stocks. Here's a bit more about two broad categories of assets—in the language of investing, these are "asset classes"—that you can hold via your index funds. When the robo investment platform is designing a portfolio for you, it will be aiming to give you a good mixture of index funds, each one holding a different kind of asset.

Stocks

Stocks are a particularly volatile, or risky, asset class. Every day, many times a day, stock prices move up and down in response to the bidding and trading of shares based on information about the company and its place in the market. If you buy a share of Apple, remember that there is an investor out there, probably a professional or a computer, selling you a share. And that investor is making an equally valid bet (and probably a much better informed one because this is their job) that Apple is going to release a dud product next quarter.

(*Continued*)

The world steadily spins off events that affect a lot of stock prices at once, such as global pandemics, and events that affect only one company dramatically. These can range from a scientist's eureka moment in the shower to nose-biting incidents. Yes. For real. In September 2022, a top executive from Beyond Meat was arrested for biting a man's nose at a University of Arkansas football game. The company's stock price sank from about $24 down to $14.50 at the end of September.

Bonds and Dividend Stocks

A bond is a less volatile kind of asset, so bond index funds are in turn less likely to go up and down rapidly (though some do). Governments issue bonds to finance building things, such as sewer systems and schools. Universities issue bonds. And companies issue bonds, too. Most of the time, they're more mature companies with slower growth rates but steadier profits than the companies issuing shares of stock. Some examples of big companies in the bond markets are Kroger, a grocery store, Boeing, an airplane manufacturer, and McDonalds, the fast-food franchise company.

Like bonds, some stocks produce regular amounts of cash: We call those dividend stocks. After a company has fairly predictable earnings, it may promise investors dividends as an additional incentive for people to buy the stock. With a dividend stock, similar to a bond, your return comes from the increase in stock price and the dividends. Bonds and dividend stocks are often lumped together because of the role they play in your portfolio. Their prices are less volatile, so they balance growth stocks.

Language of Investing

Index ETFs: Exchange-traded index funds. Robo platforms typically use index ETFs (exchange-traded funds) to build your portfolio. Index ETFs can be traded throughout the day in the markets, as opposed to index mutual funds, which are only traded at the end of the day. Index ETFs usually have slightly lower fees than index mutual funds.

Registered investment advisors (RIAs): Investment professionals regulated by the Securities and Exchange Commission who have a fiduciary duty to put their clients' interests first. Because of the higher standard, they are empowered to make more investment decisions for their clients. They're usually paid a small percentage of your portfolio.

(*Continued*)

Stockbrokers: Investment professionals regulated by the Financial Industry Regulatory Authority, a government-authorized nonprofit. Stockbrokers buy and sell investments for clients. They are paid by brokerage firms, often by commission.

Asset managers: The companies that create and manage funds. Some employ stockbrokers or registered investment advisors.

Fiduciary duty: Registered investment advisors must exercise loyalty and care to their clients. The standard imposes upon the advisor the "affirmative duty of 'utmost good faith' and full and fair disclosure of material facts" as part of loyalty and care. This includes "an obligation not to subordinate the clients' interests to its own."

Conflicts of interest: The tension created when a professional's interests (often financial) runs counter to a clients' interests. The fiduciary standard requires RIAs to disclose conflicts of interest.

Index revolution: The movement starting in the 1970s to invest in asset classes through low-cost index funds.

APIs: Application programming interface.

The Philosophy of Robo Investment Advice: Avoid the Gimmicks, Embrace the Science

RESEARCHERS ESTIMATE ABOUT 110 billion people have ever lived on planet Earth.[1] Every single one of these people has something in common: they all died or are headed in that direction. That doesn't stop people from trying to beat the odds. Chinese emperors hired alchemists to cook immortality medicine thousands of years ago. Alchemists tried to create the philosopher's stone. Today, tech moguls inject plasma extracted from young people's blood, believing it to be the liquid gold of a fountain of youth.

We know a lot about tech moguls' crazy anti-aging regimens, because we live in an age of information saturation. Some are swallowing dozens of pills every day, eating a strict diet of pureed vegetables, working their cores with muscle stimulation machines (equivalent to 20,000 sit-ups), wearing blue-light-blocking goggles for two hours before bedtime to optimize sleep quality, and engaging in various other biohacking experiments. If people are extremely wealthy, they can afford to spend a lot of money on their quests. Maybe someday, they will succeed. Does that mean you should replicate tech moguls' anti-aging regimens? And can you?

The answer is no and no. You shouldn't replicate tech moguls' anti-aging regimen, because it is yet to be scientifically validated. Researchers have made breakthrough progress in the anti-aging field in the last decades, but there is still no robust conclusion nor consensus in the scientific community on how to halt or reverse the aging process in human beings. Even if a regimen were proven, you can't afford its multi-million-dollar price tag.

The Long-Term Regimen

If you want to be physically healthy and increase your life span, you don't want tech moguls' expensive, complicated yet dubious anti-aging regimen. You need a health regimen that's proven to be effective: eat a well-balanced diet, exercise regularly, avoid addictive substances, limit alcohol, and sleep well. You will die one day, but you are more likely to live comfortably and happily into old age, spending time on the things that matter to you. If you're reading this book, we hope you're already putting in the work to be physically healthy.*

The good news is that it is even easier to adopt a healthy approach to your finances than it is to adopt a healthy approach to diet and exercise. Physical health takes constant, if low-level, discipline. Financial health takes almost no discipline at all, especially if you use a robo investment platform. They've taken over the day-to-day work of investing for the long term. All you need to do is take some basic, regular actions, such as setting up repeating bank transfers, checking on your accounts a few times a year, and filing your annual tax forms.

In the investment world, the equivalent to the diet-exercise formula for physical health is a formula that consists

---

*Nobody's perfect, but we know you're doing great! Keep going.

of diversification, keeping fees low, and minimizing your taxes. This approach has been proven to work in the long term, and it's the central message of our book.

Don't try to beat the market, invest for the long term, and use a robo platform to optimize for what you can control: diversify to reduce your risk, keep fees low, and minimize your taxes.

However, to be a successful robo investor, it's important to give up some huge misconceptions—for good.[†] This is the finance-world equivalent of following tech moguls in their crazy quest to live forever.

Misconception #3: You, a typical investor, can beat the market.

Misconception #4: You can beat the market over the long term by recognizing great buys in individual stocks or funds.

[†] Giving up the illusion of beating the market means ignoring a lot of financial media. Take a look sometime at the companies that advertise on financial websites: many are expensive mutual fund companies! Meanwhile, many people get a voyeuristic thrill from hearing about the extremely wealthy. Some wealthy people indulge in novel and fancy activities in pursuit of unattainable goals, and they get loads of attention for this dubious behavior. Tech moguls' anti-aging regime we wrote about in this chapter, a typical example, is both dubious and inaccessible.

Misconception #5: You can beat the market by figuring out which way it is heading and "timing" the market.

These are the most dangerous misconceptions in our book, because they are so damaging and so prevalent. Most people recognize that the market is hard to beat, but they don't recognize that the chances of beating the market are vanishingly small, like the chance of living beyond 120 years. And because many people overestimate their own capabilities, they believe they will be among the rare people, that they will be *the one* who beats the odds. When hubris meets desire, people have a nearly infinite capacity to believe what they want to believe.

If you're an overconfident investor laboring under the misconception that you can beat the market, you're likely to trade too often and make investments that are too risky. There's a flip side of the overconfidence, as well. Because the myth of beating the market is so prevalent, some would-be investors don't ever start investing. When the bar is set impossibly high, smart people approach the game with justifiable skepticism. If you're a skeptical investor, you're likely to invest too little or not at all.

The indexing pioneers we talked about in the last chapter recognized the futility of trying to beat the market. Robo investment platforms took their philosophy and built on it. If you're going to use these platforms to make money in your sleep, understand and embrace the underlying philosophy.

Giving Up the Illusion of Control Is Hard

"Always go to other people's funerals, otherwise they won't come to yours."

—Yogi Berra

We wrote in Chapter 1 about the thousands of stocks available to trade. That's a pretty big temptation. Misguided people still try to beat the market, and they trade individual stocks or invest in actively managed funds. After years of talking to friends about investing (and sometimes yielding to temptation ourselves), we believe that trying to beat the market is the investment world equivalent of maintaining the illusion of control in a situation where your control is limited at best. If you're a human, yielding control is always hard. Even grappling with the idea of losing control is hard, which is why it takes a minute for most people to see through Yogi Berra's play on words.[‡]

Listen, it's not just us telling you the impossibility of beating the market. Here's one of the many scientific studies that

---

[‡] Berra, like all of the Greatest Generation, grappled with reality early. He fought on D-Day during World War II, survived, went on to play for the New York Yankees, and became a manager and coach.

proves the point. Over the 20 years ending in December 2021, fewer than 10% of active US stock funds beat their benchmarks, according to S&P Dow Jones Indices.[2] What are the chances that you will pick one of the 10% and be invested in it during the right, lucky 10-year span? Vanishingly small.

In 2022, researchers did a follow-up study to the 20-year one. They looked at the 2,132 broad, actively managed stock mutual funds as of June 2018. They picked the top 25% of the funds based on their performance over the 12 months through June 2018, and followed them for the next four years, through June 2022. Not a single one of them—and remember, these were the *top* mutual funds in 2018—was able to stay in the top 25% of performance, and only 1% remained in the top 50%.

These actively managed mutual funds are managed by professional investors, with the fanciest finance degrees, aided by the richest datasets and the fastest computers. They're highly skilled and informed, and yet, they underperform the market. Would you rather try to beat the market and end up almost inevitably underperforming it, or would you rather match the market's returns? The answer should be obvious.

The Robo Investment Platform Formula

So you're not going to beat the market. What's next? This is the good part—we're going to explain how the robo

investment makes money for you. Robo Investment plat
forms put a three-pronged strategy on autopilot for the
long term.

1. Diversify to reduce risk;
2. Keep the fees low; and
3. Minimize your taxes.

Invest for the Long Term: Make Time Your Ally

"You either die young or you get older."

—Helen Mirren, actress

The poker stakes of investing the robo way is investing for
the long term. Helen Mirren, an actress still at work in her late
70s, has spoken a lot about embracing each age of her life and
been applauded for looking naturally beautiful in each one.
Rather than fighting the aging process, she learned to see time
as an ally to reinvent herself and learn more about her craft.
Other women, from Kate Winslet to Taylor Swift, demonstrate
the dual power of being yourself and staying in the game.

*"According to my birth certificate, I turn 30 this year. It's weird
because part of me still feels 18 and part of me feels 283, but the
actual age I currently am is 29."*

—Taylor Swift

Whether her age is 18, 29, 30, or 283 doesn't really matter. Taylor Swift is already an immortal in the music industry and even more so in the eyes of her fans. Qian's niece, a 14-year-old fangirl, proclaimed, "Taylor is ageless!"

These successful women's secret is they take the time to know who they are and what they want at every age. They use time to build their careers, the same way you are going to use time to build your portfolio. As an investor, you may be tempted to see time as your enemy—as in, you don't have enough of it. In every financial situation, look for a way to make time your ally. Hold your investments longer. Use long-term debt when the interest rate is lower than the inflation rate. Push off paying taxes. Wait for the market to rebound. Stick to your plan.

Investing Is the Only Way to Beat Inflation

The post-pandemic era saw the return of inflation, which makes investing for the long term even more important. Inflation is the rate at which prices increase. It can take a huge bite out of your income and your wealth if you're not careful. If you purchased an item in 1970 for $100, by 2000, that same item would have cost you more than $450.[3] Government officials hope to keep the long-term inflation rate under 2%, but some experts expect it will remain higher than that, 3–4%.[4] That means, you need to aim to achieve a higher return than 4% in your long-term savings, just to stay ahead of inflation.

We wrote earlier about the rate of return in the stock market. Over the past 50 years, 1973–2022, the US stock market returned an average of 11.7% per year, and the US bond market returned an average of 6.6% per year. These rates of return work like magic in your portfolio if you leave your money and your earnings in the market over time.

If you invest and earn 7% per year, which is a more moderate return assumption for US stocks, on your $100,000 investment, you'll have $107,000 by the second year. That year, you're earning 7% on $107,000, which gives you $114,490. In year three, you earn more than $8,000 and have $122,504— and so on. Assuming you invest $100K in an investment with 7% annual return for 30 years to fund your retirement and you pay zero fees, you will end up with $761K. It is a massive wealth accumulation that feels like magic thanks to the power of compounding. You take advantage of these rates of return and the power of compounding with one simple strategy: stay invested steadily, for as long as you can.

Sorry, Timing the Market Doesn't Work, Either

But, we hear some people saying, "Any amount of risk makes me uncomfortable." And some others are saying, "I'm not a stock picker, but I can figure out how to invest in the rising market and sell just before it starts to fall and jump quickly back in as it starts to rise."

A Bank of America study released in 2021 put this idea to rest. An investor who missed the S&P 500's 10 best days in each decade since 1930 would have earned a total return of 28%. The investor who held steady through the ups and downs would have earned 17,715%.[5]

Respectfully, we say the voice that urges you to time the market is not based on wisdom or science but is rather your very human desire to try the impossible, to control the markets. The philosophy of the robo investment platforms is different. You can't beat the market. But **you can do well by relaxing, investing for the long term, and controlling what you can control: use a robo investment platform to diversify, pay lower fees, and minimize taxes.**

This three-pronged approach to investing is better (in most respects) than what the millionaires were using before the invention of robo investment platforms because it's less expensive and more accessible. That explains why some of Wealthfront's earliest customers were Silicon Valley millionaire millennials—they recognized a good deal when they saw it.

Of course, there have been bad years. Bear markets, when stocks and bonds are declining, have lasted on average a little less than two years. In the worst one, stocks dropped

50%, though 20% is more typical. Most of the time, you can ride out a decline. It's a decline in the number that you see when you look at your account, but it's not permanent unless you hit the sell button. And, over time, based on what's happened in the past, you should see the value of your investments climb back to the previous level and then surpass it. Remember the yo-yo from Chapter 1? You're holding a yo-yo as you walk up a hill. There are a lot of ups and downs along the way, but you are trending up in general and will end up in a higher position at the end.

But still, even the most brilliant and emotionally mature investor lives with a certain amount of anxiety. You need faith to stay invested and trust that the market is going to go back up. That's why we say using a robo investment platform is not just a formula: it means adopting a philosophy of trusting research and believing that time is on your side.

If you use them wisely, robo investment platforms lower the risk you'll be caught in need of your cash at a time when the bear is raging. That's part two of the formula: diversify and de-risk.

Diversification. The robo investing platforms put into place a lot of what traditional investment advisors did, especially when it comes to diversification and crafting the right investment mix for you. (They didn't replace everything—and in Chapter 13, we'll talk about some of the emotional support and services that only humans can provide, and which some investors want and value.) Using software, the robo platforms automate portfolio design, using index funds (which are themselves diversified) to represent a diversified set of asset classes. The robo platforms are great at what's arguably the hardest part of investing: sticking to a plan, in all its mathematical detail. They don't have emotions, so they're not going to sell in a panic, or buy out of greed. You can always override them—but they're designed to remind you of what the evidence shows: don't try to beat the market. Control what you can control. Stay invested.

Low fees. At the same time, the robo investment platforms charge fees that are a lot lower than human advisors. A typical traditional advisor charges approximately 1% of the portfolio value under their care every year. That adds up to a lot. If the market returns 7% per year, and a human advisor takes a 1% slice—well, you can do the math. And in a bad year, if you lose money, you're still paying the 1%, which takes your loss down to, for example −11% from −10%. The yearly fees are high. They're downright hard to swallow if you look at them over time. If you have a portfolio of $100,000 with a human advisor, a 1% fee is $1,000 a year. Over 20 years, that's $66,000 (assuming 7% annual return before the fee)—money that you could have kept investing.

Keep tax bills low. A few years after they launched, robo investment platforms began adding automated services to lower your taxes, which they call "tax-loss harvesting."[§] What this means in plain English is that they save you a lot of money on your tax bills. Traditional investment advisors offered tax-loss harvesting, too, but they did it using spreadsheets and usually charged extra for it. And because it was manual and complicated, they didn't always do it well.

The robo investment platforms lowered the fees in every way. Their basic portfolios use low-cost ETFs. Their management fees are low, usually less than half a percent. Tax-loss harvesting is less expensive, too. True to the robo investors' roots in the index fund revolution, the platforms put high-quality, scientifically proven investing in the hands of typical investors.

These three pillars, diversification, low fees, and low tax bills, are scientifically proven to mitigate risks and drive returns in your portfolio. Investment comes with risks. Think of any investment as a package of risk and return, which always show up as a pair. You need to take risks to be rewarded with returns, and diversification can help you reduce the risks. Once you learn about these pillars, including the concepts of return and risk, by reading Chapters 4, 5, and 6, you will grasp how the robo investment platforms work, and you'll be more likely to be able to embrace the philosophy and stay the course if the market shifts.

[§]Qian designed the first version of the feature that the other robo investment platforms used as a base.

Relax and Do Less

You're most likely to achieve both physical health and financial health by relaxing a little bit. When it comes to your physical health, it's about feeling energetic at every age. When it comes to financial health, it's about meeting your goals. The good news for new investors is that financial health is a lot easier to achieve than physical health. It takes discipline and meaningful effort every day to be physically healthy, which isn't easy for any mortal. You might slip by indulging yourself with french fries, being too busy or lazy to exercise, downing four martinis with a good friend at a bar,** or getting lousy sleep because you scroll on TikTok or Instagram until 2 a.m.

Financial health, on the other hand, is automated and made easy for you by robo platforms. The platforms have the utmost discipline to execute what they are programmed to do, rain or shine, sad or happy. They also offer cash accounts, which enable you to establish and earn interest as an emergency savings account. They offer different kinds of investment accounts that help you meet your individual goals—including retirement, college saving, and taxable investment accounts. The software protects you, to some extent, from your worst impulse when you have a knee-jerk

---

** Full confession: we did this while writing the *Little Book* you are reading.

reaction that might otherwise spur you to make the worst move for your money at the worst time. They remind you that time is on your side.

Relax, invest for the long term, and control what you can control. You're not going to live forever or become a tech mogul, but you will have a great chance of living happier and healthier, with the money you need to meet your goals.

In the next three chapters, we'll go over these three things you can control, **diversification, low fees, and low tax bills** in more detail. If you understand them on a high level, you can use the robo investment platforms most effectively to build your wealth.

Key Takeaways in This Chapter

1. You can't beat the market by trading individual stocks or by timing the rise and fall of the market. Research shows even the smartest professional investors couldn't do it consistently.
2. If you relax and take a long-term approach, you will make money over time.
3. The three strategies used by robo investment platforms are diversification, keeping fees low, and minimizing investment taxes.
4. Robo investment platforms put these scientific strategies in place for you automatically.

Language of Investing

Inflation: The rate of price increase of goods and services. High inflation means the prices of goods and services are increasing rapidly. When the inflation is high, with the same amount of money, you can only buy a smaller quantity of goods and services.

The market: The aggregation of investments of a particular type in a specific region or country. In the US the market typically refers to the aggregation of publicly traded stocks and is represented by the S&P 500 index, a hypothetical portfolio holding the largest 500 publicly traded stocks in the US.

Actively managed stock mutual fund: A mutual fund with the objective to outperform the market. The fund's manager picks and invests in stocks that they believe will outperform the market. The S&P 500 index, which represents the market, is typically the benchmark to compare the fund's performance against.

Beat the market: Outperform the market. For example, outperform the S&P 500 index.

Time the market: Choose the time to invest cash in (buy) or pull cash out of (sell) the market.

Diversify: Hold a number of different investments in a portfolio to reduce risks.

Fee: The price charged by investment companies or professionals, typically expressed as a percentage of the assets under the management of the companies or professionals per year.

Section Two

What the
Platforms Do

Chapter Four

Diversify and De-risk Investments

—— ∼ ——

W E BOTH LOVE TO hike. Qian often goes to the mountains above Lake Tahoe, where the wide variety of pine species gives the trails a butterscotch scent, and she can see the cobalt lake reflecting the wide California sky. Elizabeth travels to the Bob Marshall Wilderness of Montana in the company of an outfitting family, the Cheffs. One night, the lead guide, Mark Cheff, was awakened in the middle of the night by a strange sound in the cook tent. He took the flashlight from the shelf above his bed and shined it toward the communal dining table. The grizzly licking the butter bar lifted its head and looked at Mark straight in the eye. Grabbing his .45, Mark ran out the back and headed round the side toward the front; the grizzly ran out the front and headed round the side toward the back. Man and bear met again. Then Mark shot into the air, and the bear disappeared for good.[*]

Bear markets are a lot like the butter bear of Montana: you can't avoid the bear, but if you're smart about it—and prepared—you'll walk away from the encounter just fine.

Misconception #6: A bear market will kill you.

Fear of the bear—the risk that the market will dive—is one of the biggest reasons some people don't invest. They cut themselves off from the incredible possibility of making money in their sleep because they're worried about the risk. Fortunately, robo investment platforms use a set of unparalleled tools for managing risk. In this chapter, we're going to tell you about them, so that when you do meet the bear, you

---

[*]Elizabeth wrote about this experience with 406 Wilderness Outfitters originally in an article for *Forbes*: Elizabeth MacBride, "What Happens When an Eastern Greenhorn Rides into the Wilderness with a Famous Montana Outfitter," *Forbes*, August 19, 2019, https://www.forbes.com/sites/elizabethmacbride/2018/08/19/why-we-ride-unarmed-into-the-bob-marshall-wilderness/?sh=5013d6451dfe.

can keep a cool head. The biggest mistake investors make is selling when the market declines.

Robo investment platforms protect your investments with a combination of three tools, which are all about managing risks: broad diversification, asset allocation, and rebalancing. A good way to think about this is to think about a forest. Around Lake Tahoe where Qian hikes, there are at least six pine species alone: the Jeffrey, the Ponderosa, the Sugar Pine, the Western White Pine, the Lodgepole, and the Whitebark—and some other species of trees, too, like the Quaking Aspen. The diversity confers many benefits, making the forest more efficient, as the trees occupy different layers in the canopy, more resistant to disease and pests, and more able to withstand climate change.

When you grow a forest, you want to plant diverse trees. When you create a portfolio, you want to own diversified investments because a diversified portfolio has a better chance of withstanding a variety of risks in the economy and market than a single investment, not unlike a forest has a better chance to survive pests, disease, and climate change than a single tree.

Diversification in Action

Here's a simple example of what it means to diversify in a portfolio.

The video rental company Blockbuster was a successful company in the 1990s. At the peak of its business in the late 1990s, the company had more than 9,000
stores and 65 million registered customers in the United
States. Each store was designed with open floor shelves
stocked with every VHS tape and DVD you ever heard
of. Blockbuster even pioneered a computer system tracking which customer rented what and who was late returning. However if you had only owned Blockbuster's stock
in your portfolio and held it through 2010 you would have
lost all your money.

That's because another company came along with a business consumers liked better: Netflix. Technological change is
an ever-present risk and opportunity for companies. Netflix,
founded in 1997, invented the e-commerce model of DVD
rentals and shipped your favorite titles to your home without
you having to visit a physical store and sorting through a sea
of DVDs on the shelves. Netflix also got rid of the late fees
charged by Blockbuster and hated by consumers. Blockbuster
filed for bankruptcy in 2010, after the financial crisis acceler-
ated its demise. All its stockholders were wiped out.

If you had owned a single stock, Blockbuster, you
would have lost all your money when its stock price
dropped to $0 in 2010. However, if you had owned two
stocks, Blockbuster and Netflix, guess how you would have
fared? Suppose you had invested a total of $1,000, $500 in

Blockbuster and $500 in Netflix, in May 2002 when Netflix became a publicly traded company. In July 2010 when Blockbuster's stock was delisted following its bankruptcy, your $500 investment in Blockbuster would have become $0. Yikes! Good news though—your $500 investment in Netflix would have grown to about $6,900 as its stock price grew phenomenally by 13.8x. Your two-stock portfolio would have grown from the original $1,000 to $6,900, or by 6.9x (very impressive return!), even though one of the two stocks in the portfolio went bust.

If you owned an index fund diversifying across the entire US stock market, which included both Blockbuster and Netflix, and thousands of other stocks, you would have been protected from the downside risk of any one individual stock, offset by the upside potential of others.

Robo investment platforms use index funds in the form of ETFs as the main building blocks of your portfolio. (They also offer the chance for investors to add individual stocks, but we're sticking to the basics now.) Index funds will capture the overall growth of the stock market in your portfolio, by owning the market. You'll also follow the market down, and you'll follow it up—but over time, as long as you believe in the long-term growth of the economy—it'll be up more than it's down, like the yo-yo in your hand moving up the hill.

How Scary Are Bear Markets?

Most people define a bear market as an average decline across a wide swath of the market—say, the S&P 500 or the Russell 2000—of 20% or more. If you're invested in broad-based index funds and a bear market happens, your portfolio will decline, too. But bear markets are not as scary as they seem, when you know the facts.

If you had owned an S&P 500 index fund, which holds the largest 500 stocks in the US stock market, in 2008 and 2022, the two worst bear-market years in the last 20 years, you would have lost 37% in 2008 and 18% in 2022. It certainly hurts to lose 37% or 18% in a single year, but your portfolio will not be wiped out.

Diversification will help reduce losses when some businesses or even a large swath of the economy are in distress. Just like in a forest where some trees die and the others thrive, in your diversified portfolio some investments fizzle out, for example Blockbuster, while the others take off, Netflix being a case in point. Another example is the year of 2008. The stocks in the financial sector collectively lost more than 50% of their value in 2008 as a number of large financial institutions crumbled in the financial crisis. Meanwhile the stocks in the health care sector grew by about 5%. Your index fund of tracking the largest 500 stocks would have owned the largest stocks in both sectors and the health care stocks would have softened the blow from the stocks in the financial sector.

Markets have always recovered from bear markets. Bears are followed by bulls. There have been about 12 bear markets since 1965. The average time to recover from the bear markets of 1965–2019 was 654 days, or less than two years.[1] Your portfolio loss in a bear market is only paper loss. If you don't sell, you won't have a real loss. When the next bull comes, and it always comes after a bear, your portfolio will recover. You just need to stay patient and stay invested and wait for the bull to come.

If you're in a diversified investment portfolio at a robo investment platform, you need to take only two additional steps to prepare for and then cope with a bear market:

1. Don't sell. Don't panic.
2. Make sure you have enough cash on hand to meet your needs while you wait for the market to recover. We'll talk more about your own personal risk tolerance in Section 3 of this book, but for most people we recommend an emergency account of six months of expenses. If you're expecting to make a big purchase, such as paying for college or a house in the next few years, you'd need more cash or cash-equivalent investments on hand.

We recognize this is easier said than done. Robo Investment platforms have a good track record of helping investors keep their money invested through market downturns.
When you click withdraw, you'll usually see a reminder of
the importance of staying invested. But you have to do your
part too: if the market is diving, take a deep breath. If you
have enough cash and income to see beyond the bear, history tells us that your portfolio will recover.

Asset Allocation Takes Diversification to the Next Level

Robo platforms diversify your portfolio in another way. They
sort index funds into categories, called asset classes. An asset
class is a category of similar investments. For example, all the
stocks traded on US markets are categorized as the US stocks
asset class. All the bonds issued by the federal government
as well as the state and local governments are categorized
as the US government bonds asset class. If you think of the
US stocks asset class as the pine tree species, an individual
stock is equivalent to an individual pine tree. The US
government bonds asset class is to the aspen tree species as
an individual bond to an individual aspen tree.

There's no universally agreed-upon taxonomy of asset
classes. But robo investment platforms typically diversify
across 5–10 asset classes. US stocks, US government bonds,

US corporate bonds, international stocks, and real estate investment trusts (REITs) are common asset classes. Some platforms break US stocks into more granular asset classes, for example, US large-cap stocks, US mid-cap stocks, and US small-cap stocks, according to the sizes of the businesses. Some platforms consolidate more granular asset classes into a single broader one. For example, US government bonds and US corporate bonds can be consolidated into a broader asset class, US bonds.

Asset classes offer another way to diversify your portfolio. In some markets, one asset class might decline sharply—such as stocks—while another rises—bonds being the usual example. At some moments in history, investors flee the higher volatility of stocks and race to the perceived security of US government bonds. The asset classes do produce attractive long-term returns in your portfolio but on a one-year basis (one year is short term in investing) it is impossible to predict which asset class would produce the highest return or a positive return.[2] The highest-performing asset class last year is seldom if ever the highest performing one the following year. The Callan Institute, an investment research firm, ranks nine major asset classes based on their returns every year for the 20 years during 2003–2022. The following chart illustrates the highest-performing asset class for each of the 20 years. It would have been perfect to hold the highest-performing asset class each year in a portfolio. However

Highest-Performing Asset Class per Year 2003–2022

2003	2004	2005	2006	2007
Emerging market stocks	Real estate	Emerging market stocks	Real estate	Emerging market stocks

2008	2009	2010	2011	2012
US bonds	Emerging market stocks	US small-cap stocks	US bonds	Real estate

2013	2014	2015	2016	2017
US small-cap stocks	Real estate	US large-cap stocks	US small-cap stocks	Emerging market stocks

2018	2019	2020	2021	2022
Cash equivalent	US large-cap stocks	US small-cap stocks	US large-cap stocks	Cash equivalent

Source: Adapted from The Callan Periodic Table of Investment Returns: Year-End 2022

there was no obvious pattern to predict which asset class tops the ranking each year. No asset class produced the highest return two years in a row for the 20 years. The only way to capture the highest-performing asset class is to diversify across asset classes such that when an asset class produces the highest return, it is in your portfolio.

Robo investment platforms customize your portfolio using asset classes because they offer a way to customize to your situation. When you sign up for your platform, you'll fill out a risk assessment questionnaire. If you're a 22-year-old investing for retirement, you have decades to recover from a bear market, so the platform designs a portfolio for you that includes more volatile asset classes—which also have a greater chance of rising over time. Some robo platforms, in addition to enabling people to buy individual stocks, enable people to customize portfolios by adding index funds and even asset classes. Instead, stick to the basic model the platform designs for you. Statistically speaking, it has the best chance of the highest return at a risk you can tolerate.

Robo platforms' diversification strategy has two levels—the asset class and the securities level. The platforms diversify your money across 5–10 asset classes. The index fund diversifies your money across thousands of securities within the asset class. When you invest on a platform, you own tens of thousands of securities across 5–10 asset classes, as if you own a forest of a big handful of species and tens of thousands of individual trees. The forest, like your portfolio, is healthy.

The Most Disciplined Rebalancers

Different types of trees grow organically at different rates. If left unattended, the faster-growing trees will dominate the forest while the slower-growing ones will be crowded out. Mechanical thinning, a process to remove some trees with heavy equipment, is one important tool in forest management. Thinning maintains a healthy distribution. (Nature has its own thinning mechanisms, too: wildfires.)

Different asset classes grow organically at different rates in a portfolio. If left unattended the faster-growing asset classes will dwarf the slower-growing asset classes, which would make the portfolio substantially different from and riskier than its original shape. Rebalancing is a process to shift some money from the faster-growing asset classes to the slower-growing ones to maintain the original shape of the portfolio and thus its original risk profile

This is another key advantage of a robo investment platform. It can rebalance your portfolio automatically, efficiently, and with more discipline than any human could muster. That discipline applied to the turmoil of the market means you always stick to the intended asset allocation and take the intended amount of risk, not being carried away by the market. Rebalancing is primarily a risk management tool. Research shows disciplined rebalancing improves risk-adjusted returns, meaning higher return for the same amount of risk, compared to no rebalancing.[3]

Here's how it plays out in action.

Imagine you start with a portfolio of $1,000 with a 60-40 asset allocation between US stocks and US bonds. In other words, you've invested $600 in US stocks and $400 in US bonds (this would be a bare-bones portfolio, one meant for someone willing to take average risk, who wants the simplest asset allocation).

Suppose that during the following 12 months, US stocks grew by 20% while US bonds grew by 5%. By the end of the 12 months, you end up with $720 in US stocks and $420 in US bonds, and thus the proportion becomes 63-37, which, if left unattended, is meaningfully different from and has higher risk than the original 60-40 proportion.

The difference between the actual asset allocation, 63-37, and the intended asset allocation, 60-40, is called "drift." Drifts happen all the time due to market fluctuations where asset classes ebb and flow. Robo investing platforms monitor the drift in your portfolio and rebalance the asset classes back to the original proportion periodically. In this example, the platforms will sell some US stocks and buy some US bonds to get the proportion back to 60-40. A more advanced rebalancing algorithm will use the portfolio's income (dividend or interest) to buy US bonds without selling US stocks. The purpose is to maintain your portfolio's amount of risk at 60-40, not 63-37, which is a riskier portfolio due to its higher allocation to the more volatile asset class of US stocks.

Robo investing platforms routinely monitor all the asset classes in your portfolio and rebalance them back to the intended proportion. They maintain the intended amount of risk, a task that would be difficult for a human investor and probably an impossible one to do with perfect discipline.

An advanced robo investing platform scans the asset classes in your portfolio every day. If it detects drift, it will spit out precise sell orders across some asset classes and buy orders across the other asset classes. After the sell orders and buy orders are executed and settled, the asset classes in your portfolio will return to the original proportion and amount of risk. The most advanced robo platforms use dividends to buy under-allocated asset classes without having to sell over-allocated asset classes, thus minimizing capital gain taxes (which you will learn more about in Chapter 6) in taxable accounts.

Let the Rebalancing Happen—Don't Time the Market

In the above simple portfolio example with only two asset classes, US stocks and US bonds with a 60-40 split, we assumed US stocks produce a sizable positive return of 20% in one year, which is common. What if, instead, US stocks decline by 30% in a year? That has happened in history. You will end up with $420 in US stocks and $420 in US bonds, assuming the latter still returns 5% in a year. Your portfolio has lost some of the $1,000 value it had in the beginning, about 16%, but not the full 30% loss that affected the US stocks asset class.

The stock market losing 30% in a year is a nerve-racking experience, often associated with even more anxiety-provoking news about the reality or possibility of a recession. Individual investors, rattled by the uncertainty, tend to react on their worst impulse and sell the stocks in their portfolios, which means they have assets sitting in cash.

The Problem with Timing the Market

When the stock market rebounds from the bottom, investors feel more optimistic and re-enter the market by buying stocks. This behavior is called "timing the market." Some people do it intentionally, others unintentionally. But no one in the investment world, not even the smartest professionals, has been able to consistently time the market successfully.

The typical investor underperforms the market, doing worse during bull markets *and* bear markets, because they pull money out when the market is falling and wait too long to put money in. Over the 30 years during 1993–2022, the average equity fund investor underperformed the S&P 500 by as much as 2.8% per year, according to the research firm Dalbar.[4] This was because the investors tried to time the market and guessed wrong. If you miss a handful of the market's best days, you miss a lot of the gains.[5]

Timing the market turns time into your enemy. If you make time your ally, you'll hold onto your investments for the long run. Robo platforms help you stick to the plan and control your feelings so they don't derail your portfolio

Key Takeaways in This Chapter

1. Bear markets are not *too* scary if you stay calm and have a scientifically designed portfolio.

2. Robo investment platforms diversify your portfolio through index funds. Diversification protects you from the downside risk of individual stocks.

3. Robo investment platforms use asset allocation to further diversify. A variety of asset classes also provides the foundation for customizing your portfolio, which we'll talk about in the second half of the book.

4. Robo platforms are stellar at rebalancing, which restores the asset allocation and readies your portfolio to capture the upsides of the market swings.

5. The combination of diversification, asset allocation, and rebalancing gives you the best chance of a good return for the amount of risk you are willing and comfortable taking in your allotted time frame, if you stick to the plan.

Chapter Five

Increase Your Return over Time with Lower Fees

～

On a recent chilly summer day, as we were working on this book, Qian rolled off her US 101 exit on her way to work in Northern California and noticed two gas stations. On one corner, Chevron sold regular gas for $4.89 per gallon, 12% more expensive than $4.35 per gallon charged by A&A Gas on the opposite side of the street.

Who would refuel their car at Chevron when its smaller competitor A&A Gas across the street is 12% cheaper, and why? Apart from Chevron being a more famous brand, the products sold by the two companies are basically the same. Yet, some people obviously do pay the higher price. They're wooed by the big brand, not paying that much attention, or they didn't do the math to figure out that a 54-cent difference for a 25-gallon tank is almost $15.

Unfortunately, a lot of investors, like a lot of drivers, don't pay nearly enough attention. As in the case of the gas prices, that could be because the fees in investing are described in increments or percentages, which are hard to understand. Some of the fees and costs are downright hidden. It adds up to one of the most frustrating misconceptions in investing:

Misconception #7: You're not paying investment fees, or they're so small they don't make a difference anyway.

Not true! If you fall prey to this misconception, you will pay much more than you need to. If you're a typical investor, the fees will cost you tens of thousands of dollars over your lifetime. Yes. Really. Tens of thousands of dollars. Maybe even more. If you use a robo investment platform instead of a traditional financial advisor, you could save more than $100,000 over the life of your portfolio, in lower advisory fees and lower fund fees.

Here's the truth: When you buy a bond or stock, invest in a mutual fund, or transfer money to financial advisors to manage, you buy products and services, just as when you buy gas at a gas station. You pay for investment products and services, whether you realize it or not, and because you tend to hire investment companies for a long time, the fees add up a lot.

In this chapter, we're going to talk about why robo investment platforms are a good solution for the perennial problem of investment fees. In fact, robo investment platforms shine in the low-cost category. Robo investment platforms charge less to manage your portfolio and use lower-cost funds—the index ETFs we talked about in Chapter 2. But there are differences among the robo investment platforms—some are less scrupulous than others, and some companies position themselves as online investment advisors when they're really brokerages. You need to learn to be a smart shopper in investing, as you are in other areas of your life.

How to Think about Fees

Investments with zero cost only exist in a fantasy land. Investments come with a real cost, and rightly so. People deserve to be paid fairly for their work, whether they are humans running robo platforms, human investment advisors, or the managers of mutual funds.

Companies in the financial ecosystem provide infrastructure and services to create the market and enable investors to invest in the market. Some companies slice the ownership of a large business into shares that can be purchased by small investors. Some stand in the middle of the market to match buy orders with sell orders so shares can change hands smoothly. Some develop software to match buy orders with sell orders automatically and blazingly fast. Some package a basket of stocks into a fund such that a small investor can own a basket of stocks by buying one share of the fund. It is fair for companies to charge fees for their infrastructure and services that constitute the fabric of the financial ecosystem.

You should expect to pay some fees. But you should also work to minimize them and do the kind of smart shopping and critical thinking you use when you are buying gas, a flight ticket, dance lessons for your kid, or a washing machine.

Robo Platforms Are Low Cost

From the get-go, robo investment platforms embraced the low-cost philosophy for three reasons. First of all, they were trying to sell themselves as alternatives to human advisors, and the lower fee was a selling point. Second, because they use technology to deliver their service at a much lower cost, they could pass along some of their savings to their customers. They positioned themselves as value providers, to appeal to a large number of middle-class customers and aim for profit created from scale. If human investment advisors are like Bergdorf Goodman, serving a small number of rich customers, robo platforms are like Target, serving a large number of middle-class customers (or frugal millionaires!).

And third, and most important from your perspective, the people who designed the robo investment platforms knew that high fees would create a huge drag on customers' investment performance. If your investment advisor is deducting thousands of dollars in fees from your account each year instead of prompting you to keep investing, your portfolio is growing slower than it otherwise might. Delivering better performance leads to more referrals, which creates a virtuous cycle.

Robo platforms charge low fees, typically under 0.35% per year, much lower than 1% per year charged by most human financial advisors. Assuming a robo platform charges 0.25%, or 25 bps (basis points), per year (one bp or one basis point is one percent of one percent, or 0.0001) and you invest $10,000 on the platform, you pay $10,000 × 0.0025 / 12 = $2 per month. Having your money managed by the best-in-class software implementing a proven investment strategy for a monthly fee equal to the cost of a cup of coffee is a bargain. The platforms are willing and able to charge meaningfully lower platform fees than human financial advisors thanks to software's cost and scaling advantage

How Much of a Difference Does the Lower Fee Make?

Traditional investment advisors typically charge 1% on your portfolio value per year. Though that sounds small, it's really a lot. Because of the power of compounding, smart shopping makes a huge difference over time.

Assuming you invest $100K in a portfolio with 7% annual return for 30 years to fund your retirement and you pay zero fees, you will end up with $761K. But investing for free only happens in a fantasy land—companies charge for their services.

If you pay 0.25%, or 25 bps, to the robo investment advisor every year, you will end up with $710K. You pay a total cost of $51K, compared to the fantastical no-cost ending balance of $761K. Clearly, $710K is still a massive wealth accumulation from a $100K investment, for a very reasonable total cost of $51K spanning over 30 years, or about $140 per month, which is comparable to your monthly car insurance premium. But if you pay a 1% annual fee, a typical fee charged by traditional investment advisors, which is four times 0.25% but still feels like a very small number, can you guess your ending balance after 30 years?

You will end up with $574K, which is $136K lower than the ending balance of $710K in the scenario of 0.25% annual fee! You will end up with $136K less because you paid an extra fee over 30 years. Given the US annual median household income in 2021 was about $70K, the $136K extra fee means a household losing its total income for two years!

The Other Big Fee: Fund Fees

You also pay fees for the funds in your portfolio. Each fund has a different fee, or "expense ratio" in industry jargon. The funds you own don't send you a bill in the mail for this fee—instead, it's regularly deducted from the funds' balances, for the fund managers' effort of managing the funds. Every fund is required by regulation to disclose its expense ratio, which you can look up by browsing the fund's website or reading its fund prospectus, a document explaining the fund's nuts and bolts. Realistically, very few investors take either of these two steps. Most robo platforms make it easier to see your funds' fees in their user interfaces. Robo platforms usually use low-cost index funds to construct portfolios.

Your typical fund portfolio managed by a robo platform might look like this:

Fund name	Ticker	Expense ratio as of summer 2023
Vanguard Total Stock Market ETF	VTI	0.03%
Vanguard Tax-Exempt Bond Index ETF	VTEB	0.05%
Vanguard FTSE Developed Market ETF	VEA	0.05%
Vanguard FTSE Emerging Market ETF	VWO	0.08%
Vanguard Dividend Appreciation ETF	VIG	0.06%

You can usually find the fund fees by clicking the names of them in the list of funds in your robo investment account. Many of the funds on robo platforms are exchange-traded funds (ETFs), whose expense ratios are typically under 0.15%, some of the lowest in the fund industry.

Hidden Fees in Finance

It may surprise you to learn that there are other hidden fees that come along with mutual funds, which are not reported in their expense ratios. For instance, some mutual funds pay a commission to the person selling you the fund; that commission—a hidden fee—shows up in your cost, but it might not be obvious to you. We talked about this in Chapter 2, when we talked about the business models of stockbrokers.

Actively managed mutual funds—as opposed to the index funds used by the robo investment platforms—are also notoriously tax inefficient. In an active fund, the fund manager seeks to beat the market by identifying companies that will outperform the market's consensus financial projections. The fund manager often trades stocks in and out of the fund, realizing taxable capital gains, in many cases short-term capital gains, which are taxed at a higher rate. These taxes show up in your cost. In an index fund, the fund manager seeks to replicate an index and doesn't trade as often as an active fund. Less trading means less realized capital gains, which means less tax you need to pay and more money kept in your account.

Index ETFs used by most robo platforms are even more tax efficient than index mutual funds. When an investor sells an index mutual fund's shares, the fund manager needs to sell stocks to raise cash. The selling creates realized capital gains for the fund, and the resulting taxes are borne by all the investors of the fund. When an investor sells an ETF's shares, he or she sells to another investor in the market. There is no stock selling involved in the fund, and thus it doesn't realize capital gains or tax burden to the fund's other investors.

You can track down these hidden fees and the taxes paid by reading a mutual fund prospectus. But realistically, who is going to do that? If you bring up either expense ratios or hidden cost to someone who believes in the ability of actively managed funds or stock brokers to beat the market, they'll typically say something like this: the higher returns make up for the higher expenses.

The problem is that, over time, they never do.

Does Expensive Mean Better? No. Cheap Means Good in Investing!

If you have ever been to a country club golf course, you have probably met a number of golf-playing "investment guys," who work for Wall Street firms. They buy rounds of drinks and if you meet them later in their offices, they are ready with nice sales pitches and stacks of paperwork, to sign on new clients. Investment professionals who are licensed as stockbrokers but offer what they call financial advice are the worst of all worlds. They sell their services for a high fee, usually 1% or higher on your portfolio, and they find ways to charge commissions and hidden fees as they sell you mutual funds. They market their services based on the idea that their advice is better and that they will help you beat the market. Lots of people have an "investment guy" who delivers them "great, market-beating returns" by picking stocks or buying funds.

Maybe. The problem is that the research says the opposite. Many extensive studies have established that it's not "investment guys" but low fees that drive good investment returns.

Morningstar regularly researches and reports the relationship between mutual funds' expense ratios and their returns. In the 2022 release of their annual "Mind the Gap" research report,[1] they ranked US equity mutual funds, including index funds, by their expense ratios into five equal-sized groups. They found the funds in the lowest-expense-ratio group returned 16.17% annually for the 10-year period ending 2021, while the funds in the highest-expense-ratio group returned 15.06%. The difference of more than 1% per year, seemingly small, is actually significant and would produce a huge impact to your wealth, as illustrated in the earlier hypothetical example of fees. Morningstar conducts the research using the same methodology every year for every 10-year period. Although the return gaps are different for each 10-year period, the pattern of low-expense-ratio funds significantly overperforming high-expense-ratio funds is consistent.

Cheap Means Good but Free Is Suspect

You know the old amusement park game of whack-a-mole? Investment fees, even at the robo investment platforms, are a lot like the mole. You think you've gotten rid of the mole, but the truth is that he's going to pop up again in another location. As large companies and more brokers have begun offering online investment advice and services, there is more room for the whack-a-mole behavior.

A company that offers a robo investment platform for a very low or no advisory fee may be making up for the lost revenue by offering you high-priced funds in your portfolio. Subtle differences in user interfaces might encourage you to trade, if the company is a platform where trading fees are the profit center. Some companies offer free trading but charge you money every time you withdraw from your account.

In the past few years, many financial companies have begun to offer trading for free, or no commissions. The bad news here is that they're usually making up the money by monetizing somewhere else at your expense. If you are not paying for a product, you are the product. That's why we say the most important rule to remember is: in investing, cheap means good, but free is suspect.

Key Takeaways in This Chapter

1. Lower fees mean higher returns for you.
2. Robo investment platforms were built to keep fees low.
3. Investment companies are masters at whack-a-mole: cheap means good, but free is suspect.

Robo Investing Platforms vs. Other Kinds of Investing

In this book, we outline a common-sense, emotionally nuanced approach to investing using a low-cost robo investment platform. We believe this is the best option for everyday investors today. But there are other popular approaches to investing, some better than others. They include target-date funds, DIY trading apps, and traditional financial advisors. Here's why our approach on a robo platform comes out ahead:

Target-Date Funds

Like a portfolio on a robo investment platform, these funds include a mix of funds representing different asset classes; the mix changes over time to offer lower-risk bonds as you approach retirement. Robo investment platforms represent an advance on target-date funds in five ways:

1. The basic or classic services on robo investment platforms are about the same or a little less expensive than target-date funds, on average, and you get a lot more for your money. The overall median gross expense ratio on target-date funds was 0.59%, according to a study published by the Department of Labor in 2017,[2] though others from Vanguard, are less expensive. You can expect to pay less than 0.35% on a robo investment platform for the combination of the advisory fee plus the expense ratios on its underlying index funds.

2. Rebalancing on a robo investment platform is better than in a target-date fund because it happens more frequently with software.

3. A target-date fund is just a fund. A robo investment platform gives you access to financial planning tools and a holistic view of your finances, and it will offer innovations and new features as you advance as an investor (though you should be a smart consumer about when to take advantage of new features).

(Continued)

4. Tax-loss harvesting is unavailable in target-date funds.

5. Target-date funds use fewer asset classes than most robo investment platforms.

Trading Apps

Trading apps enable you to buy individual company stocks and bonds, and funds. They operate online, and in some cases, they look a lot like robo investment platforms. They differ in a few important ways:

1. Cost and transparency. Trading apps are free, whereas robo investment platforms charge a fee, usually totaling less than 0.35% including the portfolio construction and maintenance and the underlying fund fees. Robo investment platforms have more transparent fees and business models because they're more regulated. It's hard to tell how trading apps make money. In investing, cheap is good, but free is suspect.

2. Trading vs. buy-and-hold. This is the fundamental difference between trading apps and robo investment platforms. Trading apps are built on the idea that you can make money by buying the "right" stocks or funds and selling them at the "right" time, which research has demonstrated is impossible over the long term; robo investment platforms are built on the idea that you invest in a mix of asset

classes for a long time to take advantage of the growth of the world economy. Most trading app users only trade a dozen individual stocks in the US market, which results in under-diversification.

3. Optimized portfolios. You could theoretically use a no-commission trading app to construct a good portfolio for yourself, similar to the ones you see on a robo investment platform. But it's impossible for you to optimize the portfolio the same way a robo investment platform will: you won't rebalance it daily, and you probably won't stick to your long-term asset allocation. The number one mistake investors make is trading too often. The second biggest mistake investors make is getting the timing wrong when they trade. You're more likely to do both those things on a trading app.

4. If you use a trading app, you will almost certainly incur tax gains and losses. But unlike on a robo investment platform, you won't have a method to systematically reduce the taxable gains with the losses. (We're going to talk more about tax-loss harvesting in the next chapter.)

Traditional Financial Advisors

Traditional financial advisors and robo investment platforms offer many of the same services, including portfolio design

(*Continued*)

and maintenance and financial planning services. There are three big differences:

1. Personalization/perks. Basic robo investment platforms offer some level of personalization, but some traditional financial advisors go a step further, with services such as phone calls to reassure you when the market is falling. Some offer perks—such as tickets to events and dinners, though those aren't really investment services. Some robo investment platforms offer access to personal advisors for a higher account minimum or higher fee.

2. Cost. In general, robo investment platforms are much less expensive, with advisory fees of 0.35% or less (and some platforms offer their services for no fee at all). Traditional financial advisors typically charge 1%.

3. Optimization. It's impossible for humans to do some investment tasks at the level that robo investment platforms do, such as daily rebalancing and tax-loss harvesting.

Chapter Six

Lower Tax Bills

~

A COUPLE OF YEARS AGO, Elizabeth's older daughter, Lillie, went off to college, driving her first car, a small blue used Mazda she nicknamed Milo. About six months later, she got an envelope in the mail: the city of Alexandria, Virginia, had a car tax, and it was going to cost Lillie $136.

"This is terrible news," she texted her mother, aghast.

Yep. Despite all the good things that we get from taxes—roads, water and sewer, schools, and our social safety net—it feels like a real blow when you discover all the multitudes of ways local, state, and federal governments tax you and how much you're paying. So we're sorry to tell you now that we have to debunk another common misconception about investing:

Misconception #8: You don't pay taxes on money you make from investing.

Many people believe they don't pay taxes on investment income, or they may be vaguely aware they pay taxes but assume they have no control over how much or when they pay. This misconception may spring up because most people invest only through their retirement accounts, which are tax-deferred. (It also comes as terrible news to some people that the income they draw from their retirement savings in a traditional IRA or a 401(k) after they retire is taxed. Sooner or later, the government gets its share.)

As we'll explain in this chapter, you do pay taxes when you make money from investing, but robo investment platforms can reduce those taxes more effectively than other strategies.

Robo investment platforms are particularly good at minimizing taxes because of their long-term approach to investing, which makes it easy to save for retirement. Their user interfaces and easy automation keep you focused on saving regularly over the long term and encourage you not to cash out.

Some robo investment platforms also offer a strategy called tax-loss harvesting, which Wealthfront pioneered. We expect that more platforms will follow suit in this competitive industry.[*] Tax-loss harvesting gives most investors who use it a $3,000 deduction to take against their regular income tax and some investors with larger portfolios, more. For a family being taxed at a 24% marginal tax rate, a $3,000 deduction against their income is a saving of more than $700 annually, enough to cover annual fees that typical robo investment platforms charge, multiple times over.

You don't need to be a sophisticated investor to use a tax-loss harvesting service, but you do need a taxable investment account. But even if you're just starting out as an investor and are focused on building up your tax-deferred retirement accounts, it pays to understand this chapter and the long-term benefit of tax efficiency, in your retirement accounts and your taxable accounts.

In this chapter, we're going to go over seven separate topics:

Leaving Your Money in the Market Is a Good Tax Strategy
Tax-Deferred (Retirement and College Savings) Accounts

---

[*] As of this writing in summer 2023, four robo investment platforms offer tax-loss harvesting: Axos Investing, Betterment, Empower, and Wealthfront. Vanguard Digital Advisor plans to add the service, based on press reports.

Investing in General Is a Good Tax Strategy
Avoid the Temptation to Cash Out
Minimize Taxes as the Wealthy Do
How Tax-Loss Harvesting Works on Robo Platforms
How Robo Platforms Help you at Tax-Filing Time

Leaving Your Money in the Market Is a Good Tax Strategy

If the terrible news about investing is that you do pay taxes, the corresponding good news is that you pay the taxes only when you make money, and usually only when you sell your investments. The exception to this is that you pay taxes on the dividends and interest you get from dividend-paying stocks and interest-producing bonds, even when you don't sell the underlying stock or bond. Generally, however, the ability to wait on selling your investments gives you a lot of control—not only over when you pay but over how much you pay.

You want to minimize your taxes because, well, don't we all want to minimize our taxes, as long as we're staying within the rules? You especially want to minimize your investment taxes for the same reason you want to limit your fees: because in investing, over time, little bits make a big difference. If you save $1,000 on the taxes on your investment income, that's an extra $1,000 you keep investing and compounding.

Robo investment platforms help you minimize your tax bills in two ways:

- Tax-deferred accounts, such as IRAs and 529 Plans for college saving; and
- Tax-loss harvesting in taxable accounts.

Remember, in investing, one of the most important rules is to turn time into your ally. Both of these strategies rely on what's called the time value of money. When you put paying taxes off into the future, you almost always make more money over the long term, because you leave more money in the market to grow and compound. Over the long term, taxes deferred means money gained.

Tax-Deferred Accounts

If you participate in a really great 401(k) plan at work or you're one of the very few workers that still has a pension, you might not have to worry about retirement savings as much. About 69% of American private industry workers and 92% of public workers have access to retirement plans at work.[1] **If you have a 401(k) plan at work, where your employer matches your contributions, you should max out the match. That's free money, and there's no better deal in investing.**

After you establish an emergency account and max out your 401(k) match, you can open an individual retirement account. There are three basic kinds of individual retirement accounts: traditional IRAs, Roth IRAs, and SEP (Simplified Employee Pension) IRAs. Robo investment platforms' low-cost index funds and orientation toward the long term mean robo investing is particularly well-suited to retirement saving.

However, be aware of the income limits on deductions. In 2023, the IRS phased out the deductibility of IRA contributions for households earning more than $136,000 a year, where one of the spouses was covered by a 401(k).[†] You can still save in an IRA, but you can't deduct the contribution, or you can opt for a Roth IRA, which also has no deduction but slightly different rules.

If you don't have a 401(k) or you do with an income below the deductible limit, you can save money and take a deduction from your annual income taxes with either a traditional or SEP IRA. There's a great tax benefit to this: if you earn $120,000 a year and save $6,500 in a traditional IRA, your taxable income drops to $113,500. If you're staying

---

[†] The IRS website is surprisingly easy to search and use. The deduction rules, which unfortunately change often, can be found with a search of the keywords "IRA deduction limits."

home with caregiving duties, set up an IRA for yourself. You can't afford to give up these years of compounding.[‡]

Traditional IRAs work well for people who have jobs (inside or outside the home) but may not be covered by a retirement plan. Robo investment platforms also offer SEP IRAs, which have higher contribution limits and are best for self-employed people and small business owners with no or very few employees. Robos also offer Roth IRAs, which are after-tax accounts that have more flexible rules for withdrawing money tax-free. You don't take a deduction on contributions to your Roth IRA. Because you pay taxes on your contributions to a Roth IRA before you deposit the money, you don't have to pay once you start withdrawing.

To bring the time value of this tax deferral home, consider that if you invest $100,000 in a bond fund that pays $5,000 interest in one year, you'd owe $1,200 in taxes on the interest assuming 24% marginal income tax rate, if the money were growing in a taxable account. However, in an IRA, where tax is deferred, you get to keep the $1,200 in your account and let it grow and compound.

[‡] And: don't leave investment decisions in the hands of your spouse! This kind of decision can come back to hurt in the case of a divorce, with women who have more often sacrificed careers to stay home on the losing end of the financial settlement.

IRAs are an important tax-deferred tool in the American retirement system, and we will discuss them more in Chapter 10. There are other tax-deferred accounts available on most robo investment platforms, such as 529 plans, which enable you to save for college.

Investing in General Is a Good Tax Strategy

That brings us to taxable accounts. After you've funded your retirement accounts, start saving for goals such as buying a house or graduate school or supplementing retirement income. We want you to take advantage of the higher returns that come from investing, rather than just saving. You might be surprised to learn that the federal government offers incentives to invest in non-retirement accounts, too.

The US government and most state governments generally favor the gains you earn by investing long term in the market, so they tax it at lower rates. The idea is that the US economy will grow faster and stronger, overall, if companies can count on having enough capital, either via selling stock or issuing bonds, for a long time, to invest in new business ideas.

Here's how the incentives work for you in a hypothetical example. If you make a $100,000 salary as an auto mechanic, a teacher, or an accountant, you will pay income taxes (after deductions). The current marginal tax rate for families making $100,000 is 24%. Say you got an inheritance from your grandmother of $100,000, which you invest in a diversified portfolio of stocks. Over the next 12 months, it gains $7,000 in value from price appreciation. If you cash out sometime in the first year, you'll pay taxes at your marginal rate, 24%, on the $7,000 gain. But as long as you wait at least a year to cash out, the government will tax your $7,000 gain at a lower rate, called long-term capital gains tax rate. For most investors, including the mechanic making $100,000 annual salary in our hypothetical example, the long-term capital gains rate is only 15% (lower than their marginal income tax rate of 24%). In some cases, the long-term capital gains tax rate is 0% for low-income investors.

Another type of investment income that has different tax rates depending on time is dividends, issued by stocks or stock funds. Stock dividends are a regular payment of a portion of the issuing company's profit to its shareholders. For example, the chocolate company Hershey (HSY) and pharmaceutical company Merck (MRK) pay quarterly dividends from their steady profit (apparently, we can add medicine and chocolate to the certainties in life, along with death and taxes). A stock fund, which holds a basket of stocks, aggregates each stock's dividend and pays out the lump sum as the fund's dividend to its shareholders. When you receive a dividend either from a stock or stock fund in a taxable account, you make investment income in the form of dividend, which is taxable. If you have held the stock or stock fund for a specified minimum period of time—usually a couple of months—the dividend you receive is called a qualified dividend, which is taxed at the long-term capital gains rate (15% for the hypothetical mechanic in the previous example). Otherwise, it is called an ordinary dividend, which is taxed at your income tax rate (24% for the hypothetical mechanic in the previous example), higher than your long-term capital gains rate (15%).

You can avoid paying taxes on price appreciation by holding on to your investments, because you only get taxed when you cash out. You cannot delay paying taxes on dividends, but you can lower the tax rate by holding dividend-paying stock funds for the long term, and again make time your ally.

Avoid the Temptation to Cash Out

By now, it should be obvious that investing for the long term is a great way to minimize taxes. This has a positive effect overall on your portfolio because the money you leave in the market continues to grow, compounding over time. Stay invested and don't cash out to take your gains. We know it can be tempting to cash out from your house or graduate school fund and even your retirement account.

It's also tempting to eat french fries, drink martinis, and buy fun clothes. A good robo investment platform is sort of like a weight loss coach: it will have a user interface that reminds you of the high cost of cashing out, which is the investment world equivalent of cheating on your diet. In the second half of this book, we'll talk about how to handle those kinds of temptations—it's not by denying them all. Just as when you diet, it's all about moderation. But for now, we're getting the basics down. And the basic rule is: keep your money in the market. You'll pay lower taxes and make more money.

Now we come to the crown jewel of robo investment platforms: tax-loss harvesting. So far, we've been talking about how to defer taxes by taking retirement deductions and leaving your money in the market long term. But it turns out that there's another way you can lower your tax bills when you lose money in the market. Yep, that's right, a loss can be a good thing in the investment world. And guess what? The constant buying and selling on an automated robo investment platform to keep you diversified generates another benefit: losses that you never see in your bottom line but that can lower your taxes.

Minimize Taxes as the Wealthy Do

One of the widely known secrets of the US tax code is that it favors investors over workers. That favoritism is one of the big reasons the wealthiest Americans pay lower tax rates than middle-class and upper middle class families; the wealthy earn more money from investments than labor. Middle-class and upper middle–class families pay about 9–14% of their income as taxes to the government (after deductions) while the wealthiest 400 American families pay only about 8% of their income as taxes, according to a 2021 study by the White House Council of Economic Advisors.[2]

The wealthy also use a strategy called tax-loss harvesting. This strategy, which sells losing investments to realize capital losses to reduce tax bills, has been employed by traditional financial advisors manually for their wealthy clients for decades.

We typically harvest fruit, crops, vegetables, success, or profit, something of value. A loss typically isn't of any value. However, in the investing world, realized capital losses can be used to offset realized capital gains to reduce tax bills. The tax bill reduction, or tax savings, permissible by the tax code, is the value harvested by tax-loss harvesting. Robo platforms codified tax-loss harvesting's mechanics into software to detect and harvest opportunities in each asset class when the market ebbs and flows. They brought the coveted strategy to everyone.

In the introduction, Elizabeth and Qian disclosed we have estimated tax savings of $1,100[§] and $5,200 in our

---

[§] Elizabeth's taxable portfolio is fairly small.

taxable accounts, respectively. The amount is estimated as the realized short-term losses multiplied by our short-term capital gain tax rate, plus the realized long-term losses multiplied by our long-term capital gain tax rate, and reported to us individually as the estimated benefit of the tax-loss harvesting feature in our taxable accounts. Results for individual investors vary, depending on the size and volatility of your portfolio and the tax rate you pay. But most investors using tax-loss harvesting will have an extra $3,000 deduction to take annually against their ordinary income, even if they don't itemize.

How Tax-Loss Harvesting Works on Robo Platforms

To understand tax-loss harvesting, you need to first understand diversification (which you do, because you read Chapter 4, top-to-bottom!). You know that your portfolio consists of multiple low-cost index ETFs and those funds trade like stocks on the market, their prices rising and falling each day.

The tax-loss harvesting software sells the funds that have decreased in value. The software uses the proceeds from the sale to buy a similar index ETF to maintain the risk-and-return characteristics of the portfolio. Remember the importance of staying balanced from the chapter on diversification? If your funds are sold for less than you paid, the sales realize capital losses. You'll use those losses to offset the realized capital gains on other taxable investments you report to the IRS. Here's a simple example of how tax-loss harvesting works in your portfolio.[3] We'll follow up with an explanation of how it works on your income tax return.

Imagine that you have a portfolio that includes SPY (this is an ETF that tracks the performance of the S&P 500 index). If you bought a share of SPY for $200, and one day, the price fell to $150, you could sell your share of SPY, harvest the $50 loss, and purchase a new ETF to replace it.

To abide by federal law and to maintain the risk profile of your portfolio, this new ETF needs to meet several criteria. First, it needs to be *different enough* that the transaction isn't considered a "wash sale" (more on that later). This means it needs to track a different index than your original ETF does. Second, it's important that this ETF is *similar enough* that your portfolio still maintains the same risk and return characteristics. This means it should be highly correlated with the original ETF so your portfolio's level of risk doesn't get out of whack.

In this example, let's say you decide to replace your share of SPY with VONE, an ETF that tracks the performance of the Russell 1000 index. This index's performance is highly correlated with the performance of the S&P 500, but it's different enough that SPY sales shouldn't be considered a wash sale.

LOWER TAX BILLS   [111]

If you bought VONE to replace the SPY shares you sold, you'd still have a diversified portfolio with roughly the same level of risk. And, of course, you would have harvested a $50 capital loss, which can be used to offset realized capital gains. Hypothetically, if you have $50 realized capital gain from another investment, it will be wiped out by the $50 realized capital loss. On a net basis you have zero capital gain and would pay zero taxes, instead of paying taxes on the $50 realized capital gain.

Does it feel as if you're putting one over on the IRS by doing this? You're not. The rules are designed to keep people from buying and selling the same securities over and over again as they gain or lose value, which would disrupt the market. The IRS rules exist so that there's no tax code incentive for those kinds of shenanigans. In the previous example, if you sell SPY at $150 (when the original purchase price was $200) and buy it back within 30 days, the sale is a wash sale and the $50 realized capital loss cannot be used to offset realized capital gains. That's why robo platforms will replace SPY with a similar but different ETF—so as to avoid making wash sales.

The most advanced robo platforms use two or three highly correlated ETFs for each asset class and rotate your money among them to capture harvesting opportunities while staying clear of the wash sale caveat. Similar to rebalancing, robo platforms detect opportunities and execute trades daily so you don't have to. Because robo platforms are software-based, they are able to make the complicated calculations and trades required for tax-loss harvesting at scale at a low cost to investors.

It's important to note here that some traditional investment advisors have criticized tax-loss harvesting; we suspect this is because they can't do it as efficiently as robo investment platforms with the best software. If you've been following along closely in this chapter—and kudos to you, by the way, for endeavoring to understand America's tax policy—you might have a question about what happens eventually in your portfolio. You're swapping out index funds to take advantage of short-term losses, but eventually, if you sell some or all of your portfolio, you will pay a capital gains tax on the index fund that is the last fund standing in your portfolio. But remember, the long-term capital gains tax is lower than your ordinary income tax. And you might not ever sell it, or you might sell it when tax rates are lower or higher. Tax rates are unfortunately difficult to predict (tax rates are set in Washington, DC, an inherently unpredictable place), so it's better to take the deduction when you can.

Wealthfront reports its tax-loss harvesting results each year by producing a number it calls the "harvesting yield," which measures the quantity of harvested losses (short or long term) during a given period, multiplied by tax rates, divided by the value of the portfolio, at the beginning of the period. The results depend on an individual portfolio's size, its volatility (portfolios with more volatility produce more losses that can be harvested), and the federal tax rates individual families pay.

The industry would do well to adopt Wealthfront's transparency. As tax efficiency becomes a more important aspect of investing, we expect tax-loss harvesting will become a more common feature on all the robo investment platforms, and therefore an area of intense competition. Not all tax-loss harvesting software is the same, and the results can differ between them. We'll go over this more in Chapter 14, when we're talking about the features offered by the different platforms.

For most people, who don't want to take a lot of time in the weeds of tax strategies and policy, you can relax and let the robo platforms do their work. Your responsibility is only to file the paperwork, which we'll go over next.

How Robo Platforms Help You at Tax-Filing Time

Robo investment platforms issue you a Form 5498 to show your tax-deductible contributions to IRAs, just as all investment firms that offer these accounts do. Robo investment platforms that offer tax-loss harvesting also issue you a Form 1099-B to report capital gains and losses and a 1099-DIV to report dividends.

Do you always have realized capital gains, every year? Absolutely not. You do in some years and not in other years. Investing is inherently unpredictable. For the years you don't have realized capital gains, you won't be able to use the realized capital losses harvested by the robo investment platforms. That is not a problem. If you have no realized capital gains, you can use tax-loss harvesting's realized capital losses to offset, at the maximum, $3,000 of your income from a job or self-employment, which would reduce the income taxes you owe. If 24% is the marginal income tax rate you pay, called marginal tax rate, offsetting your income by $3000 would reduce your income taxes by $3000 × 24% = $720, a meaningful amount for many American families.

If you still have unused realized capital losses, meaning the remaining amount not used to offset any realized capital gains or income, you wouldn't lose them. You can carry them forward and use them to offset realized capital gains and income next year, the year after that, and any future year after that. Think of farmers who produced a fantastic harvest of grains and couldn't eat or sell them in the year. They store the unconsumed grains in a barn and use them in a future year when needs arise.

We Know This Is Really Tedious

We did our best to make this chapter on taxes easy to read, but you still may be feeling overwhelmed by myriad tedious tax rules. Capital gains could be realized or unrealized, realized capital gains could be taxed at the long-term rate or short-term rate, dividends could be qualified or ordinary and are taxed differently, realized capital losses harvested by tax-loss harvesting could offset realized capital gains and income, and . . . yada yada yada. If you are feeling overwhelmed, you are not alone. The tax code is complicated and overwhelming to everyone, not just you.

If you decide to try a robo platform this year, fast-forward to next April, the next tax-filing frenzy. You sit at your computer, trying to recall the tax rules you learned in this chapter and trying to figure out your taxes. **The good news is you don't need to do any of the stressful chores.** Your robo investment platform will keep track of these different kinds of taxable gains and losses. You use the statements it sends to fill out your returns, give it to your accountant, or you can find a robo investment platform that integrates with a common tax preparation software.

The tax preparation software will automatically import your realized capital gains and losses, dividends, and interests from your robo investment account. The tax preparation software will calculate taxes for you automatically so you don't have to wrangle complicated spreadsheets. It will even carry forward your unused realized capital losses automatically to use them in the future. You do not need to record them in a notebook or spreadsheet and then worry about forgetting where you stashed them away. Robo platforms not only make investing easy but also make tax-filing easy.

Key Takeaways in This Chapter

1. Robo investment platforms lower your tax bills by encouraging long-term investing and by making it easy to invest in tax-deferred retirement accounts.

2. Fund your retirement accounts first, resist the urge to cash out, and then set up a taxable account.

3. Robo investment platforms will harvest the losses in your taxable account to offset capital gains or income. The strategy is called tax-loss harvesting.

4. For most families paying a 24% tax rate who have a taxable account, tax-loss harvesting covers the annual fees on a typical robo investment platform, but results can vary depending on your tax rate, the size of your portfolio, and its volatility, or risk level.

5. Connect your robo investment account to your tax-preparation software and/or keep your accountant informed of the robo investment accounts and features.

Chapter Seven

Technology Brings It Home

As WE WERE IN the thick of writing the book, in July 2023, the *Barbie* movie debuted in theaters and swept audiences off their (flat) feet. Gender differences are palpable in the fantasy world of Barbieland. Barbies are gorgeous, happy, empowered, successful, and invincible. Kens, although with perfect six-pack abs, don't have their own identities other than being Barbies' boyfriends and are generally confused about life.

In the investing world, people are so accustomed to gender differences that they don't even see them. But they're real and devastating. Women do save. Unfortunately, fewer women invest than men do. (One robo investment platform, Ellevest, focuses on helping women invest, with content and a user interface geared toward women.) After a lifetime of receiving cultural messages that women are less capable of financial decisions than men, women think they don't have sufficient knowledge to invest and worry more about investment risks. They feel less comfortable and confident in investing. In the relationship-driven traditional financial advice industry, most financial advisors are male, which makes it harder for female investors to relate to them. Women's under-investment accompanied by the statistics that women tend to live longer than men creates a double whammy for women's financial security.[1]

It's not only women who encounter barriers when they reach out to become part of the investing world. People of color have encountered overt racism. Only 44% of Black American families have retirement savings accounts, and on average they own about $20,000 of stock, compared to 65% of white American families, who have an average balance of $50,000, according to the Federal Reserve. Rates of retirement savings are even lower among Hispanic families, with only 32% participating in a plan. On average, they own stock worth $14,900.[2] Middle-class people are usually excluded from high-quality personalized financial advice by the high fees and account minimums of traditional financial advisors.

Many Americans have bought into the idea that investing is only available to a select few. Luckily, this next misconception is being dispelled fast.

Misconception #9: Investors are wealthy white men.

In the past several decades, many companies have opened investing up by moving it online and making it cheaper. We talked about the index revolution and the movement toward online brokerages and free stock trading. The advent of robo investment platforms brought down one of the last barriers to investing, the high fees of quality, trustworthy financial advice. Now, high-quality advice is available and easy for almost anyone.

If you are a female reader, or a middle-class person, a young person, a person of color, or anyone feeling inadequate in your knowledge and intimidated by investing, we hope that by reading this book you will become more knowledgeable and thus more comfortable about investing. Robo investment platforms are gender-neutral. You engage with robo platforms via user interfaces on websites and mobile apps. The platforms remove the hurdle of holding uncomfortable conversations and building awkward relationships with male financial advisors. We think robo platforms contribute to closing many investing gaps.

Features That Make Investing Easy

Long-term focus. Robo platforms help turn time into your ally. These platforms have designed some of the best user interfaces to help you focus on the long term. You log in to a home page that tells you how your investments are likely to do over time toward your own financial goals. This level of personalization enables you to focus on what is important: your own portfolio and your goals, not how the market is doing lately.

Lower account minimums. Most robo investment platforms have account minimums under $5,000, and many are under $500. A few even have a $0 account minimum. The vast majority of traditional financial advisors—the ones charging 1% or more on all the assets under management—focus on serving people with more than $500,000 to invest.

Convenience. Time is money. Robo investment platforms' apps and websites enable you to make changes to your accounts or check on your balances within a few seconds. In the beginning, some experts were concerned that it would be too easy for investors to withdraw money during market downturns (remember, this is the number one mistake investors make). But that hasn't proven the case. Plus the platforms' integration with tax preparation software makes investment gain tax-filing just a click.

Personalization. The best robo investment platforms offer two levels of personalization: First, through asset allocation, they design a portfolio for you based on a risk questionnaire you fill out. Second, they adjust the portfolios over time as you age. Your portfolio should change as you get closer to retirement, with a mix of investments that is less volatile.

Personalization also includes financial planning. Robo investment platforms aren't perfect at this—there's definitely room for innovation when it comes to answering investors' questions. But many offer a variety of financial planning tools. Some of the most useful tools help you visualize whether you have enough money to retire (and help you figure out how much more you need to be saving). They may deliver a tough message about earning and saving more, but wouldn't you rather know so you can adjust your behavior when you are still young? Other tools help you plan, save, and invest for medium-term goals such as vacations, home renovations, and graduate school.

Holistic view of your finances. One of the most powerful tools in a robo investment platform is the ability to connect different parts of your financial life on your mobile app so that you can see your retirement investments in context with the value of your house, the totals in your bank accounts, and your taxable investment accounts. You can also connect family members' accounts on the platforms, which is convenient if you have aging parents or growing children and want to make sure they aren't going to run out of money.

It's hard to underestimate the value of this holistic view, especially for people who are anxious about money (which might be most of us). If the market is going down, with the tap of a few buttons, you can remind yourself of how much it went up previously. You can confirm you have a cash cushion. And you can also log in every once in a while, when the market, the value of your home, or rates on cash are going up, to remind yourself of how nice it is to make money in your sleep.

If you hate your job but you're too afraid to quit, a holistic view of your finances may tell you that you have the flexibility. On the other hand, a holistic view of your finances may tell you to hold on for a little bit longer until the right opportunity comes along.

Rapid evolution. We believe robo investment platforms' greatest value is the pillars we outlined in Section 2: diversification, low fees, and low taxes, wrapped in easy-to-use user interfaces that keep you focused on your long-term financial health. But the investment world changes quickly. Because they exist online, robo investment platforms often ship new products—such as cryptocurrency—faster than traditional financial services companies do. That's both good and bad; you need to exercise some agency to decide if a new product is right for you. On the whole, however, we think robo investment platforms' ability to add new products quickly is good.

Taking the irritation away. By making it convenient, reassuring, rewarding, and fun to look at your investments and your financial life generally, robo investment platforms make it more likely you will save what you need to for the long run. You don't need to consult financial news websites for insights on how to invest. That's a stress-inducing activity if there ever was one! You don't need to listen to your neighbors' probably fallacious fish tales about their investment prowess. If you feel the urge to compare yourself with someone else, you can just quietly log in to your app, watch your financial life clicking into place over time, and feel grateful for what you've earned and for the chance to spend it, give it away, or pass it down.

What the Wealthy Know

Elizabeth sometimes goes to a retreat in the Appalachians at a place called Shrine Mont to focus on writing projects. On one of her visits, there was a young family visiting the mountain retreat at the same time Elizabeth was there, and they were part of a church group from one of the best-endowed churches in Virginia. She heard snippets of their conversation all week and marveled at how many of them revolved around money. The parents were teaching their children how finance worked, and the adults were putting the lessons into practice in discussions about how to pay for the church's restoration. The lesson here is not about judging whether money deserves such a prominent place in a faith retreat but that among wealthy families, financial education is one of the most important lessons. It's complicated, deemed as deeply worthy, and woven into daily life, which is one reason wealthy families stay wealthy in America. Wealthy families—the wise ones—hire people to do the day-to-day work of managing their money so they can focus on the emotional aspects of personal and group finance, such as teaching their children to delay gratification or figuring out which is a higher priority between repairing a wall and building a steeple, and figuring that out in a way that keeps peace in a community.

Before robo investment platforms, wealthy families hired human investment advisors who helped them with the tedious work of investing. The robo investment platforms brought the best practices—diversified portfolios and lower taxes—home to everyone by lowering fees and account minimums. The robo platforms ended up making investing better for everyone, including the wealthy. Why would anyone pay 1% a year when you could get the same services for less than half that fee? The difference isn't just the 1% a year—it's easily tens of thousands of dollars over the life of your portfolio.

Robo investment platforms, if you find a good one and use it wisely, are built to make investing itself easy so you can focus on the complicated emotional questions and on setting the right financial goals for you. That's what we're going to talk about in the next section of the book.

Eventually, we hope you'll find yourself with the confidence to teach a child about good financial habits, such as saving to earn interest, watching out for high fees, and how to finance something good for the community. High-quality investment services and the information and wisdom to use them shouldn't be exclusive to wealthy families. Now, it's not: you're holding this *Little Book*, and the ability to start investing with confidence is only a few clicks away.

Key Takeaways in This Chapter

1. By offering high-quality financial advice at a low cost, robo investment platforms have lowered one of the last barriers to investing well.

2. A good robo investment platform is a fiduciary, like the traditional financial advisors wealthy families have been using for years. They take the grunt work off your shoulders.

3. Robo investment platforms enable you to focus on the emotions and decision-making that surrounds money, which actually is hard in some cases. They have features that help you stay focused on your own goals and financial health.

4. Pass it down! Incorporate your own knowledge about saving, investing, and finance in the lessons you teach the kids in your life.

Public Equities versus Private Equities

At this point in the book, you might be wondering: But what about famous investors who make a killing and become wealthy overnight by placing an incredibly wise bet? Is investing in the public markets "just" a science, a formula that enables me to build wealth slowly over time if I follow the rules?

The answer, basically, is yes. The reason has to do with the nature of markets, which function based on information. To make money in a market, you need access to information before other people—the ones trading across from you—do. In our current information-saturated environment, it's so hard for a typical investor to find high-quality information (that other people don't also have access to), that it's not worth trying. Those are the public markets. Public markets, as we wrote back in Chapter 1, are governed by laws that require companies to be transparent, to create a level playing field for investors.

There are many companies and investment opportunities—a growing number—that sell their shares to investors in private deals. This is the world of angel investors and venture capitalists and a few publicly accessible platforms, such as WeFunder and SeedInvest. On those platforms, you can make bets based on insights and information that aren't publicly available. But you also face the risk of too much concentration—remember, the big advantage of public markets is your ability to build a diverse portfolio in them. The rapid exchange of shares means prices are constantly being set and also that you can sell your shares. The private markets move slower, as people make bigger bets, often in the tens of thousands of dollars or more. For that reason, the US Securities and Exchange Commission has rules that mean only wealthy investors can take part in most private equity deals—because, in the private markets, the chances are high that you'll lose your money. The few winners in private markets make the headlines.

How to Use
a Robo Platform

Chapter Eight

Be Self-Aware about Money

~

A FEW YEARS AGO, ELIZABETH was working on her taxes, focusing on the section for deductions she could take for donations to charity. She wrote $1,000 down on the line next to what she'd donated to a group called Giving Grace, which helps single parents about to be evicted. When she went back to look at her credit card receipts, she realized the total was much lower: $400. What happened?

When it financial decisions, emotions cloud our rational brains, even our memories. The feeling of wanting to help

Giving Grace combined with the worry about what she could actually afford meant Elizabeth mentally gave herself credit for the act without carrying it through. In fact, our minds fool us—a lot—when it comes to money. By extension and perhaps even more so, our minds fool us when it comes to investing.

Misconception #10: People make rational decisions with their money.

If you operate under this misconception, you're likely to make emotionally driven decisions without being aware that you are. In fact, if you think of yourself as particularly rational, we wager that you are in fact *more* emotionally driven than most people. Unmanaged emotions get in the way of investing because countless financial decisions benefit from a critical view of risk and a long-term vision of the future. Becoming aware of your own emotions and assumptions and using that awareness as a tool to engage your critical mind is one key to making money in your sleep.

Over the past three decades, a growing body of research and theory has demonstrated how much, and how, our emotions, combined with the environments we're in, affect our attitudes and decisions about money. In the behavioral economics classic *Thinking, Fast and Slow*, Daniel Kahneman outlines the two systems of thinking in our human brains:

System 1, which is fast and intuitive, and System 2, which is slow and effortful: critical thinking.

People ought to make financial decisions using System 2, because the rational mind is good at predicting the future and assessing risks. But it's effortful to engage critical thinking. It's much easier to make decisions based on System 1—your intuition and what feels right. Being a good investor means doing things that feel hard and wrong, such as not panicking when the market falls or setting aside money every month you'd rather be using to take your friends to dinner.

Financial decisions land too often in the intuitive zone because your relationship with money is, mostly, not really about money. Very often, it is about something else: your dreams, fears, or anxieties. Perhaps it's about your ego and need to control, your need to keep the peace in a relationship, or your strong desire to care for your family.

Money is the economic expression of value in our society. It's hard to exert your rational brain when you have defined something as a "value." For instance, if you grew up in poverty and are determined to provide the best for your children, you may buy them an expensive gift you can't afford. That feels right. But if you engage your critical thinking skills, you realize saving money now will give you what you need in retirement so that you're not a burden on your children. Consider both ideas before you decide.

A strong feeling can be a clue to your own assumptions and unconscious drivers.

If you feel anxiety, guilt, or anger when you're buying that too-expensive gift, that could be a sign you're acting to heal an old wound. Unfortunately, the smartest people are often the most gifted at rationalizing. They rationalize their emotions, turning them into unassailable values and rules, which make it even harder for them to separate System 1 (their emotions) from System 2 (their critical minds).

Here are four examples where we have seen people make decisions unnecessarily counter to their own future financial interests.

Overspending When You're Young

A friend, Althea, between jobs, drove across the country with friends, cashing out a small balance from her retirement plan to pay for the trip. People in their 20s sometimes can't conceive of aging—which is a hard concept for everyone! When you're 25, a road trip with friends that costs $2,000 is a lot more real than the $32,000 you could have in four decades if you put the money in the market. Althea wasn't necessarily wrong for thinking in the short term—sometimes the road trip with your friends *is* the right investment. But she later regretted the decision.

We're saying: be aware of your unconscious drivers so you can weigh the short term against the long term. Are you feeling lonely or afraid that you might not have enough friends? Loneliness and fear could cloud your judgment and keep you from seeing that you could also grow your friendships by hanging out regularly in a park, or grabbing a coffee or drink a few nights a month, which might cost $500. That way, you invest the remaining $1,500 in your retirement plan this year and end up with (perhaps) $24,000.

Sometimes you might seek to fill an *emotional* need with something that can be acquired by dollars, only to feel the same emotional need return in a few weeks. We shop to get a short-term boost. Marketers have been taking advantage of that human tendency since—well—forever.

Holding On to the House

In a divorce, we have seen couples make irrational decisions around the house they bought together. Emotions lead one party to buy the other out—I want to be rid of that person forever!—when the money would be better invested in the market, not in the pocket of your ex-spouse. It's not pleasant to have your ex-spouse on the mortgage, but as long as they're not demanding the money and you keep paying the mortgage, the bank doesn't care. Sometimes we have seen a divorced person who can't afford the payments hold on to the house as a reminder of a previous, more secure life, when the more rational act would be to sell, move somewhere cheaper, and invest the money.

Paying for College Instead of Your Retirement

Lots of parents we know commit to paying for their children's college educations. This isn't always the right choice. Doing the math is hard—that's why we lean on our intuitive thinking more than our critical thinking, because the latter takes energy. But it's particularly helpful here. If you give your child $50,000 a year for a four-year college (or total of $200,000) in your late 40s, you could be giving up $774,000 in total in retirement savings down the road (assuming you invest the $200,000 in the market for 20 years at a 7% annual return). You need to weigh that against the student debt your child might acquire, probably at a 6–8% interest rate. Traditional financial advice dictates putting your retirement ahead of your kids' education because they'll have more options to make money throughout their careers than you will have in your 70s to fill a retirement shortfall. There's no right or wrong answer, but engaging your critical

BE SELF-AWARE ABOUT MONEY [137]

thinking skills might lead you to broaden the frame of the financial problem you're grappling with. A better decision might be two years of community college to lower the bill to $120,000 and then a combination of your contributions and a limited education loan.

Keeping a Job You Hate—Forever

We have both known high-powered, highly paid executives who have more than enough money to satisfy every need for the rest of their lives but keep working at jobs that they hate. They are probably making the people around them miserable. They say they're building a nest of wealth for some moment in the future that never seems to come, but they're driven by something else entirely, a need to win or to feel valuable.

Some people fear change so much they stay in a rut where they're miserable. And sometimes, money is a grand substitution for a real sense of self-worth.

One benefit of a robo investment platform is that it gives you a supportive environment and helpful tools to engage System #2, your critical thinking skills, as you set your financial goals, determine your risk level, and monitor your accounts periodically over time. But you have to be open to the challenge.

Mind Traps That Hurt Investors

Broadly speaking, men (or people with stereotypically male characteristics) tend to be overconfident in their ability to beat the market.[1] They trade more actively. More frequent trading causes them to underperform the market, which they are in denial of to protect their self-images of competence. Women (or people with stereotypically female characteristics) prioritize available resources on their loved ones over themselves, sometimes because they view themselves as less worthy, without realizing they should put on oxygen masks for themselves first before helping others. Here are a handful of mind traps that affect many people

The Illusion of Skill

In Chapter 3, we wrote about the misconception that an individual investor can beat the market consistently, over time. There's a mind trap that lies under this misconception: the illusion of skill. Kahneman writes about this particularly in one financial firm. Invited to give a talk at one wealth advisory firm, he looked at the investment outcomes of 25 wealth advisors for eight consecutive years.

> *Each adviser's score for each year was his (most of them were men) main determinant of his year-end bonus. It was a simple matter to rank the advisers by their performance in*

each year and to determine whether there were persistent differences in skill among them and whether the same advisers consistently achieved better returns for their clients year after year.

The results of his statistical analysis found that the likelihood of any advisor doing better than the others based on skill was zero. Yet, the firm paid out bonuses to the top-ranked advisor—it was rewarding luck as if it were skill. When Kahneman brought this to the management's attention, they left the bonus system intact. "Facts that challenge basic assumptions—and thereby threaten people's livelihood and self-esteem—are simply not absorbed," he writes.

We share this example in part as a reminder that beating the market over time is a matter of luck. Don't risk your money on luck. The example is also a reminder of how difficult it is for anyone to absorb information that challenges their assumptions or values. People don't want to believe that success in life is a matter of luck. For most people, it's a frightening idea. They'd rather believe in skill.

Fear of Loss

If you can see an event—such as losing your shirt in a bear market and going broke—in vivid detail, the fear produced by your imagination (System 1) interferes with your assessment of the likelihood of the event (System 2). Women are particularly prone to what some financial experts call "bag-lady syndrome." Women worry they'll go broke and not have the resources to care for their families. As we talk about in Chapter 4, the likelihood of a catastrophic loss—"losing your shirt" in a bear market—is low, especially if you have a diversified portfolio. But the likelihood of significant market downturns over your investing time frame is very high. Don't let your fear disengage your critical thinking skills and keep you from investing.

Consider what would happen if your portfolio lost 37% in value in a year and took two years to recover from the loss. That's a reasonable expectation of a worst-case scenario, based on the effect on the S&P 500 in 2008 in the depth of the Great Recession. What would happen to you in that worst-case scenario? Absolutely nothing, as long as you don't sell and have the monthly income and excess cash you need.

Engaging your critical thinking skills might also lead you to diversify even further from the S&P 500. In the Great Recession, if you had a very basic diversified portfolio of 60% in the S&P 500 and 40% in US Treasury Bonds, your loss in 2008 would have been 14%, much lower and less painful than the 37% loss incurred to the S&P 500 alone. (Remember in the difference between these scenarios: The all-stock portfolio has a higher likelihood of ending up at a higher level over decades, while the diversified portfolio will have a lower total performance and a lower volatility.)

Nothing in life is guaranteed, but you are well equipped to evaluate risk and reward if (1) you're well informed and (2) you can make financial decisions with input from both System 1 and System 2. Don't assume that just because you have a strong feeling, you won't change your mind based on a critical analysis. Do the math before you decide whether and how much to invest.

Narrow Framing

One of the biggest traps in behavioral finance is the narrow frame of a problem. We used an example of it in the question about paying for kids' college a few paragraphs above: Should you pay for a high-priced college or contribute to your retirement savings? Take a step back and frame the question broadly. How do we balance college and retirement? There are other solutions.

Financial services firms that are trying to market their services use narrow frames often. Sometimes they define a problem, such as "Stock trading is expensive!" and a solution: "We'll offer it for free." Broaden the frame and ask the question: Should I be trading stocks? Or: If this firm is offering free trades, how are they making money?

Emotional frames are common in financial services marketing. A cheerful silver-haired couple lounges lakeside. The implication: Sign up, and you will feel as happy as this couple does! The intent is to keep your decision-making within your System 1. But if you also apply System 2 (do the math!), you realize you could be paying more than 1% a year for these retirement planning services. What is the actual cost, and will there really be a higher return to justify it? We hope by this point you recognize that it is vanishingly unlikely that a traditional advisor charging 1% can justify their higher fees with higher returns.

Key Takeaways in This Chapter

1. Your emotions affect your decision-making around money. This is part of being human.
2. To make good financial decisions, you need to acknowledge your intuitive and emotional mind (System 1) and then actively engage your critical thinking skills (System 2).
3. Make yourself do the math when you make financial decisions.
4. Three particularly common mind traps that hurt investors are the illusion of skill, fear of (an unlikely very steep) loss, and narrow framing.

Chapter Nine

Investing Is Dating for the Long Term

❧

I F YOU'VE SPENT TIME on dating apps, you know how hard it is to judge a person by their profiles. The apps are great for short-term connections: you can tell whether someone is good-looking and likes to hike, dine out, or binge-watch TV. But if you want a connection that moves from the short term to the long term, you need another set of qualities entirely.

Dr. Shannon Curry, a forensic psychologist, gave us the best scientific definition of these qualities in a podcast episode.[1] For a long-term relationship, you want someone who combines the physical attraction and the full with three qualities: high on conscientiousness, low on neuroticism, and low-to-medium on novelty.

We think this is helpful to think about as you commit to staying the course on your robo investment strategy.

Misconception #11: Investing should be exciting, like day-trading or investing early in a new trend.

We humans are easily influenced by "happy hormones," such as oxytocin, dopamine, and serotonin, released by our brains when we're attracted to another person. These hormones give us a surge of positive emotions. However, they don't last long. They tend to fade after about six months, and happy hormones are not good indicators for a long-term relationship. Good indicators are the three qualities that can be loosely interpreted as (1) be responsible, (2) be calm, and (3) be fairly boring, which are also exactly what you need to successfully invest your money for the long term.

If you operate under the misconception that investing early in a new trend and/or day-trading will make you money, you'll move some of your money from your "boring" investment strategy (where it needs to stay to make money for the long term), and you'll put it in an investment that has a much higher chance of being risky or at least not well understood. You'll get hit by a double whammy—sort of like when you give up a good long-term relationship for an exciting neighbor. You'll lose out on the gains that you might have had if you kept your money in the market, and you'll be exposed to more risk than you needed to take.

Sorry. Investing can be fun if you're watching your account climb, and it can feel satisfying. But in a day-to-day sense, investing well on a robo platform trends more toward the boring.

The Novelty Trap

Tom Brady, a legendary NFL quarterback for the New England Patriots, stands in a spacious, spotless open kitchen, wearing a blue hoodie. His then-wife Gisele Bündchen, a supermodel, sits by a stunning floor-to-ceiling window. Brady dials a friend and says confidently into the phone, "I am getting into crypto with FTX. You in?"

It's a scene from a 2021 commercial for FTX, a then high-flying cryptocurrency exchange. In November 2022, FTX declared bankruptcy.[2] Its customers couldn't withdraw their money, and at least $1 billion of customer funds could not be accounted for. Sam Bankman-Fried, FTX's founder, later was arrested and charged with securities fraud and theft. Celebrities including Brady and Bündchen were named in a class action suit alleging consumer deception.[3] That year, Bitcoin, the most popular cryptocurrency, lost 60% of its value, and the crypto market in 2022 lost $2 trillion.[4]

Crypto was incredibly tempting. In fact, Elizabeth dropped some of her portfolio (2%) into crypto—and lived to regret it a couple of years later when she wanted some money from her Roth account to pay for grad school. The investments are still there, and the bear market in crypto will end—crypto might be a solid long-term bet. But she's unlikely to make up for the gains she would have experienced had she kept her money in the diversified mix of index funds recommended by robo platforms. If she does eventually make up for the losses, it'll be entirely a matter of luck.

Low-to-Medium Novelty

Many robo investment platforms include access to many different kinds of investments, including cryptocurrency and fractional shares of individual stocks, neither of which we think typical investors should add in large quantities to their portfolios.

Brain research has shown that a rush of dopamine accompanies new experiences of any kind. Basically, novelty makes us happy. We chase new things to be happy—a new lipstick, a new pair of sneakers, a new smartphone, eating at a new restaurant, traveling to a new country, or investing in a new type of investment. Besides the newness, cryptocurrency felt even more attractive to many people due to the celebrity endorsement. It's easy to fall for trading cryptocurrency on FTX if Tom Brady, whose success as an American football quarterback you have been admiring for years, asked "Crypto. FTX. You in?" The fear of missing out also contributed to the herd behavior—it is hard to hold your ground when you hear your friends talk about all the money they made trading crypto.

Any new type of investment brings much higher risks to investors because its history is too short for anyone to understand its behavior. It's also easy for fraudsters to scam money from investors because the investment isn't well understood or even regulated to protect investor interest. The likelihood is also low that you're really investing early. Most chances to invest in an innovative product and service happen in the private market, explained in Chapter 7.

That doesn't mean you can't have fun with novel investments. If experimenting makes you happy, go for it. Just limit the percentage of the portfolio you use to make those investments—we suggest under 2% of your total portfolio or under 5% of your investable assets. And recognize you're making the investment for a burst of dopamine, not because you're likely to make money.

Investment fads come and go, from the 17th-century Tulip Mania in Holland to the crypto boom and bust in the 2020s. Some of them are accompanied by serious fraudulent activities. If you are extremely knowledgeable about a new investment and can make informed investment decisions, set aside a limited amount of your portfolio. However, the majority of the people are not in a position to make informed investment decisions about new trends and would be better off staying away.

In the investing world, basic equals quality, like cheap equals good. The best robo platforms are registered investment advisors (RIAs) and have fiduciary responsibilities, meaning they are required by law to watch out for your financial interest. The portfolio is designed to shield you from investment fads. If you absolutely have to scratch the itch, the fiduciary robo platforms will allow you to play with the gimmicks up to a small percentage of your account balance, to protect you from bad outcomes.

High on Conscientiousness

The governments and your employer aren't responsible for 100% of your retirement needs, but you are. You are also responsible for the down payment for a house, college tuition for your kids, family vacations, and medical bills when someone you love is sick. If you invest with a robo platform, your part of the strategy is simple: each month, set aside the amount that you can transfer into your investment platform. Set up automatic transfers to these accounts. We suggest establishing three, in this order:

An Emergency Account for Cash

Almost all of the robo investment platforms now include cash accounts, earning robust interest rates of more than 4% annually at the time of writing, which are federally insured up to a significant amount. You can save for emergencies with these accounts. You should keep six months of expenses in this account. (If you don't use a robo investment platform, please set up an emergency account elsewhere.)

A Retirement Account(s)

Establish your retirement accounts, using the planners on the investment platforms to set the amount you should be investing monthly to reach your goal. Each time you log in, you'll see how much progress you're making toward these goals. (We talk more about the specific kinds of retirement accounts in Chapters 6 and 10.)

A Taxable Investment Account

You can establish a taxable investment account for your medium-term goals, such as a big vacation or sabbatical year, as long as the goal is at least three to five years away. (Bonds can be good choices for these accounts.) Or save more toward your retirement after you max out your retirement account contribution. Remember to watch for your tax-loss harvesting results on this account, which will be reported to you on Form 1099-B. Send that form to your accountant or your tax-planning software.

Robo platforms help you set, keep, invest toward, and track your progress toward your goals in each of these financial planning buckets. They supplement your conscientiousness. They assist you to make proactive investing choices based on proven investment strategies. They nudge you to take financial responsibilities to yourself and your loved ones seriously.

Low on Neuroticism

Neurotic people tend toward anxiety or even depression. In investing, it pays to stay calm and not to dwell on current troubles. By definition, this means going against the herd. When you are faced with depressing news and a rapidly plunging market, it's natural to feel some anxiety and fear. Humans are a social species. When everyone else is in panic, we also panic. When everyone else sells, we also want to sell.

Robo investment platforms make it harder to be a neurotic investor. Instead of overreacting to a market turndown out of fear, a robo investment platform helps you avoid the urge to sell. And then, it rebalances your portfolio by buying some US stocks and returning the asset class weights to the intended allocation. The robo platform will do this mechanically, responsibly, and consistently. You just need to stay calm and let the platform do its magic on your behalf.

Investing reminds us a lot of dating. Dating is a market matching people looking to build relationships with each other. A relationship has risks but is emotionally satisfying if it lasts long and connects two people deeply. Investing is a market matching investors with investments. An investment has risks but is financially rewarding if it creates economic value for the long term. Technology has transformed both dating and investing, often for the good—but only if you have a smart approach. The number of profiles on dating apps feels as overwhelming as the number of investments available in brokerage accounts. Dating apps have filters to help you select candidates, not unlike brokerage firms have screeners to help investors choose investments. An attractive person is a chat away, and a trade is a click away.

Even the key to creating a long-term satisfying relationship and investing success is similar—know what you are looking for before getting into the noisy markets, and make decisions using your slow and effortful System-2 brain, outlined by Daniel Kahneman and explained in Chapter 8, rather than the short-term excitement and fear your fast and intuitive System-1 brain is prone to (because you are a human). A System-2 approach in investing means using a robo investment platform.

And in dating? Next time you are on a dinner date, intoxicated by a handsome guy or a gorgeous gal, don't forget to activate your System-2 brain to analyze whether he or she has the qualities you are looking for.

Stay the Course

You'll benefit the most from a robo investment platform if you stick to your plan. This idea can be summed up in the phrase "Stay the course." Once you've invested the time to think critically about your financial goals and to set them, the next challenge, and one of the hardest, is to stick to the plan. In the many decades before robo investment platforms existed, traditional investment advisors and experts recognized our "dating" qualities as the most important factors in success. Can you resist the temptation to jump on a new bandwagon—such as the crypto one pulled along by Tom Brady? Can you stick to a regimen of regular and boring investments? And can you talk yourself out of panics that strike in a volatile market?

Return-chasing is a behavior bias where investors tend to buy more of an investment after it appreciates, which typically indicates the investors are changing their courses, responding to short-term movements of the market. Research shows that adopting robo-advising reduces individual inventors' return-chasing bias, among other well-known behavioral biases that tend to lead investors to stray away from their strategies.[5] The jury is out on how much robo investment platforms help investors avoid the novelty trap: responding to their customers, many of the platforms have added features that allow trading, and some have offered new asset classes. Fiduciary robo investment platforms will disclose the risks and provide guidance. It's up to you to read them and parse those opportunities carefully. Play with a novel investment with a small amount of money if you like, but stay the course with the body of your portfolio.

Key Takeaways in This Chapter

1. Investing is like dating: high on conscientiousness, low-to-medium on novelty and low on neuroticism are the qualities needed for long-term success.

2. Robo investment platforms rebalance and diversify with utmost discipline (they're conscientious), they limit or even exclude the amount you can stray (low-to-medium novelty), and they discourage you from panicking when the market turns down (keep calm and carry on!).

3. The long-term focus on a robo investment platform helps you resist the short-term appeal of new but unproven strategies.

Chapter Ten

Budgeting and
Wealth Building

~

Many investing books gloss over the most important precursor to investing: saving. We didn't want to do that, for two reasons. First of all, saving enough is arguably the single biggest financial challenge facing Americans today. The average American family has about $42,000 saved across all bank accounts.[1] But in young families where the heads of household are under 35, the average total was much less: $11,250. Given that you need to keep about six months of expenses in an emergency cash account, neither of these amounts is enough to start investing in the market. We want to give you some help—as much as we can in a book about investing—about how to start budgeting. Second, the question of how to save shouldn't be divorced from how to invest well: both depend on taking a long-term view. You need System 2, your rational brain, for saving and investing. Trigger warning! You will need to do some math in this chapter and the next one. We'll give you the three precursors to success on robo investment platforms: live below your means, set financial goals, and figure out your own risk tolerance.

Misconception #12: The key to saving is being frugal.

This misconception is part of a harsh mindset that runs directly counter to success on a robo investment platform. It's never about control, or going to the wire, or pushing your limits. It's about setting your own goals and building a portfolio that achieves investment returns high enough to reach your goals (with the least amount of risk possible). Robo platforms help you do this because of one of their best attributes: they are holistic. They make it easy to establish an emergency savings account and then move on to other goals. You funnel savings into multiple accounts easily, establish the right risk/reward profile for different goals, and keep track of where you stand, because the accounts are on the same platform.

To use a robo investment platform in the best possible way, you need to become a regular saver, which in turn means being able to consistently delay gratification. The key to maintaining a saving-and-investing habit is similar to the key to long-term healthy eating.

Live Below Your Means

One of the biggest misconceptions about saving is that it's about spending less. In reality, most people find it a lot easier to earn more. Since nobody is going to hand you more money, that means you need to continue advancing in your career or taking on side projects. Working as hard as you can in your younger years pays off a lot, down the road. It's easier to work hard when you're young. And putting yourself in a position to save in your 20s means you will benefit from the enormous power of compounding for a longer time. Not everyone can do it—and we sympathize with that. But we're saying: first earn as much as you reasonably can, and *then* look to create a workable budget so that you live below your means.

One easy-to-follow rule is the 50/30/20: Fifty percent of your income should go toward necessities, such as housing, food, and your car; 30% to fun items, such as movies, vacations, and dining out; and 20% to saving or reducing debt.[2]

You'll first need to track your expenses to see how close you are to 50/30/20. You can see if you're wildly out of line, which may indicate that you need a bigger lifestyle change, such as moving to a cheaper place or getting a better-paying job.

Let's run through the next steps for a person or a family making $100,000 a year. After taxes (including state and local), your income is about $70,000. Let's assume there's no 401(k) at work. After setting aside 80%, roughly $4,700 per month for expenses and lifestyle, there's about $1,200 left over each month.

You open an account at a robo investment advisor, say a high-yield cash account for emergencies and a traditional IRA, and now you go about setting up automatic transfers. But how much goes into each one?

The four most important financial goals for most Americans are:

1. Establish an emergency savings account;
2. Pay for more education to adapt to the changing economy;
3. Buy a house;
4. Retire with enough money.

Emergency Fund

The first step for everyone is to start building an emergency fund. We recommend that you keep six months of expenses for emergencies. For a person or family with $4,700 monthly expense, it would be about $28,000. However, with only $1,200 a month to save (and we're presuming that there isn't debt to pay off), it'll take a while to build the emergency savings to $28,000: almost two years. In the meantime, you're missing out on the chance to begin investing for retirement and taking advantage of compounding. If you're young, even a few years makes a big difference.

If you start saving $500 a month when you're 20 and keep going until you're 45, you'll have $405,000, assuming a 7% return per year. If you start five years later when you're 30, you'll have $260,000, which is substantially lower than $405,000. Every year you put off starting is costly.

As long as you have a steady income,* we'd suggest you split the $1,200 a month, putting $500 into an IRA and $700 a month in an emergency savings account. The single most powerful tactic for achieving these goals is setting up automatic deposits or transfers from your bank to the robo investment platform.

If you're concerned about keeping your emergency account at a robo investment platform, don't be. It's easy to pull the money back to your checking account if you need

---

* Self-employed people need to focus more on an emergency savings fund, because their income is less certain. This is highly individualized, however: a self-employed person with a rare, high-demand skill and a client base is more secure than a coding freelancer facing rising competition.

to (it takes a few days and will become instant soon thanks to technological advances). And robo investment platforms' partnering banks use the Federal Insurance Deposit Corp. to insure your cash up to $250,000. Because they often have alliances with more than one bank, some robo investment platforms can insure cash up to several multiples of $250,000.

We know it's hard to forego wants in favor of saving and investing for the future. Some finance experts have experimented with helping people imagine their future selves: when you save, you're giving your future self a level of security and comfort that isn't otherwise guaranteed. There's lots of good advice available about saving money. We think the three easiest places to economize are eating out in restaurants, cutting unnecessary subscriptions, and grocery and clothing shopping. After you've established regular savings into your emergency account, then you can think about setting aside money for other goals. The most important of these is retirement.

Robo Investment Platforms Are Great Places to Save for Retirement

You already know there's a nice tax deduction when you deposit money in individual retirement accounts such as traditional IRAs or SEP IRAs. What's more important is that the money grows tax-free over time. Remember the magic of compounding that we talked about in Chapter 2.

Assuming you (and your spouse) are not covered by workplace 401(k) plans, if you contribute $6,500 of your pretax income in a Traditional IRA on a robo investment platform, you save a nice amount on this year's tax bill. Admittedly, you don't have the money to spend, and that can hurt. If you are taxed at a 24% marginal tax rate, a $6,500 contribution to your IRA gives you an instant tax savings of $1,560.[†] But what happens next is far more powerful. If you invest $6,500 and earn an annual average of 7% a year, you'll make $455. The second year, presuming you leave the account alone and the market is still rising at 7%, you'll make $487. And every year after, you'll make more money. At the end of 20 years, you'll have a total of $25,153 pretax, and $19,116 after tax, assuming your marginal tax rate is still 24%.

Some people have a hard time putting money into retirement accounts because they feel like it'll be out of reach. But this is a situation where you should do the math to see how you make more money. If this were a taxable account, you put

---

[†] When Elizabeth was self-employed, she used to wait every year for her accountant's estimate of how much in taxes she owed; then, she'd gather up all the cash she could possibly spare and drop it into her SEP IRA to reduce the tax bill. Eventually, her income became more regular and she set aside $650 a month, which made it easier to plan and was a better investment strategy to capture returns over time in the market's volatility.

$4,940 (the amount left after you pay the income tax on the $6,500 pretax income at 24%). At an annual average return of 7% from asset price appreciation, you will make $346 for the first year and $370 the second year. You'll have a total of $19,116 pretax at the end of 20 years with $14,176 long-term capital gain. Assuming the long-term capital tax rate is 15%, you'll end up with $16,990 after tax, $2,116 lower than the $19,116 you would have gotten in a traditional IRA.

Do you remember Lillie, Elizabeth's daughter, whom you met in Chapter 6? She was upset to find out about car taxes and that the government has a way of getting its share. Is it likely that the government will forgo its share of this nice retirement portfolio you are making—and a nice investment income you are making *in your sleep*, to boot? Nope.

In the case of traditional IRAs and SEP IRAs, you will pay taxes after you retire and begin to withdraw the money. In the case of a Roth, as long as you hold the money in the account for at least five years, you won't pay taxes on the withdrawals. (The government got its share at the beginning because Roth contributions aren't deductible.)

How to Establish Your Retirement Age and Your Financial Goals

When you're establishing an investment account—a retirement or taxable account—on a robo investment platform, it will lead you through an automated exercise to determine your level of risk, which in turn determines the ideal asset allocation of your portfolio. Let's talk about goal-setting first because your financial goals determine what kinds of accounts to open and what levels of risk you need to take.

After you've built your emergency fund, set up buckets for the other big financial goals. Your bucket for retirement savings is either a traditional IRA or a SEP IRA, if you're self-employed. Remember, SEPs have a much higher contribution limit to help you save more tax-free. The amounts you save in these buckets will be determined in part by when you plan to retire. Robo investment platforms offer financial planning tools that enable you to put in different retirement ages, so you can see how much money you will have at different ages, with expected rates of return, including your Social Security payments. Even a few years can make a big difference. Remember our 10-year rule. If you have $1 million by age 60 and are invested in a good, diversified stock portfolio, consider waiting until 67: you could have closer to $1.5 million and a higher Social Security payment, to boot.[‡]

[‡] Of course, you need to consider your health. If you're brave enough, take a careful stock of life expectancies in your family and have a frank conversation with your doctor as you're making these financial decisions.

Roth IRAs can also be a good vehicle for retirement savings, if you can afford to forego the tax deduction that you'd get on a traditional or SEP plan. The big difference with a Roth is that, though you pay taxes the year you make the contribution, you never pay taxes on that money again as long as you abide by the IRS rules—not on the contributions and not on the earnings. That's in contrast to traditional or SEP IRAs: as you withdraw money from those, you will pay taxes.

Saving for Medium-Term Goals: High-Yield Savings, Roth IRAs, or Bond Accounts

If you're saving for your first house or graduate school, there are a few good options. Wealthfront offers a taxable investment account that builds a low-risk portfolio for you out of bonds. It will deliver a higher rate of return than a cash account but with a fairly low risk. It's likely other robo investment platforms will follow this offering, as they adapt to an environment with higher interest rates. You can use a bond account to save for a medium-term goal, one that is three to five years away.

A Roth IRA invested at the right level of risk (depending on how far into the future your savings goal is) is also a good vehicle to save for medium-term goals because you can get the higher returns of a diversified portfolio with a tax benefit. You don't get a tax deduction at the beginning, but your earnings grow tax-free. If you take the money out before retirement for what are called "qualified" deductions—your first house or grad school—you won't owe taxes on that money.

If your goal is one year away, a high-yield savings account is the best option. If you've been using a Roth IRA or a bond account to save for a medium-term goal that is now within a year, move the money to a savings account. That way, if there's a market downturn, you won't be caught short.

Fun Goals

A taxable investment account works well for things such as a sabbatical, buying a boat, or other fun goals (such as your dream of owning a Chanel suit[§] or a vacation home) that are five years off or more. By definition, if you've already saved for your future, this is excess money. You can afford to take a higher level of risk with it, and hope that pays off in earning a higher rate of return. Or, if you like, invest with lower risk if that makes you feel better.

Presuming that you're not going to live or die by the Chanel suit or boat (maybe you'd be OK with a used Chanel or a smaller seacraft), the choice of how much risk to take is an individual one. But slow down, and do the math. The exercise will help you figure out what to do.

[§] This is one of Qian's goals.

Investing $100 a month at a 7% rate of return means you'll have about $34,000 after 10 years. At a 4% rate of return, you'll have $29,000. At 7% (presuming you're invested in a stock portfolio), you'll face a higher risk of a bear market that puts a sizeable dent in your savings for two or three years but also a potential reward: the market could go up 10% a year during that time frame, and then you'll have more than $40,000. On the other hand, the steady 4%, which you can find in a cash or bond investment, means you can reasonably plan on a fairly certain return.

Sometime during this process of budgeting, investment allocations, and life planning, we suggest you take a step back to consider a couple of philosophical questions. It's easy to say: save 20% of your income. But you're more likely to actually do it if you have thought through some bigger questions about how you want to spend your time, when you want to retire, and how hard you want to work to generate income to invest. That's what we'll talk about in the next chapter.

Key Takeaways in This Chapter

1. Live below your means. Follow the 50/30/20 rule.
2. Establish an emergency account. Establish a retirement savings account.
3. For most people, the key to budgeting is earning more, not being frugal.

In the United States, You Are the Only One 100% Responsible for Your Retirement

The federal government takes some responsibility for providing for retirements. You contribute to the Social Security fund in the form of taxes every year and can take regular payment when you retire. In 2023, the average monthly Social Security payment was about $1,700, not enough for most retirees to live on.[3] Your employer might take some responsibility by providing a match in your 401(k), **which you should take advantage of—this is free money, an automatic return on your investment, and one of the best deals in investing.** The federal government and state and local governments provide public pensions to their workers. Public pensions typically pay a retiree about $2,000 per month, also not enough for most people to retire on. Corporations basically stopped offering pensions to their workers—only 15% of private industry workers have access to pensions.[4]

Chapter Eleven

Understand Risk and Pick the Right Risk Tolerance

~

MANY INVESTORS, ESPECIALLY SMALL and new investors, overestimate their risk tolerance. They yank their money out when the market turns downward, because they panic. Or some investors cash out their holdings in a down market because they find themselves in need of money just at the wrong time. If you invest on a robo investment platform, you can make money in your sleep. But we don't want you to *lose* sleep because you've taken so much risk that you're worried you won't have enough money.

Misconception #13: You should max out your risk profile as an investor, to earn the highest returns possible.

As you set up an investment on a robo investment platform, you'll usually be asked a series of questions to establish your *risk tolerance*. Remember the definition of risk from earlier in the book: volatility. A riskier investment has a higher potential reward over time, but it may also drop a lot in the short-term. Stocks are the riskiest asset class, and within stocks, some, such as emerging markets stocks, are considered even riskier.

Risk tolerance is a technical term that boils down to the question of how much money you can tolerate losing in a market downturn. From the perspective of a robo investment platform, "tolerate" means how much you lose before you yank your money out—a move that's bad for the platform and bad for you. From your perspective, "tolerate" means how much you can afford to lose if the loss happens when you most need the money. Many investors overestimate their risk tolerance, we believe for two reasons.

Some investors haven't bothered to think through the questions we're going to pose in this chapter. Many investors are overconfident in general. They haven't put much real thought into the hard realities of their financial lives and imagine themselves as investment superstars. This is the investment-world equivalent of the better-than-average effect, the tendency for people to see their abilities, attributes, and personality traits as superior compared with their average peers.[1] This is a mathematical impossibility.

The second reason is that people feel short of money and overestimate their risk tolerance because they believe a higher risk will lead to a greater return, fast. If you invest in a portfolio of 90% stocks, versus one of 30% stocks, the statistical probability (to a near certainty) is indeed that you will end up with a higher return for the long term. But remember, that return comes with a cost: higher volatility. At some points in your journey, your portfolio might be down—a lot—as much as 50%. It can take a few years for your portfolio to completely recover. What if the timing doesn't work out for you; what if you need, in an emergency, more than your portfolio is currently worth?

This is the complicated emotional terrain that you and your robo investment platform are navigating together. The first 12 years of robo investment platforms' history shows they're doing well at their part of the job.

How Robo Investment Platforms Assess Your Risk Tolerance

As we said, robo investment platforms typically ask all their investors to fill out short questionnaires. Some of them call these a risk tolerance questionnaire; in other cases, it's a risk profile. What a robo investment platform is driving at with its questions is one simple idea: How likely are you to pull money from the platform in the case of a market downturn? That's the single biggest mistake investors make.

With that in mind, the platforms want to know your income level and asset level, because the amount of excess cash you have helps determine, in part, how panic-prone you'll be. They'll also ask a few deeper questions, such as:

Imagine you started with a $10,000 investment. Then, in one month, your investment lost $1,000 in value. What would you do next?

Or

How much downside risk, on a sliding scale, would you be willing to take for a chance at making $300,000? An equivalent $300,000, or something less?

After a robo investment platform determines a risk tolerance score for you, it puts you into a diversified portfolio of index funds, with a higher weighting of bond funds and dividend stock funds if there's a sign—such as low income or low investable assets or high anxiety—that you will be stressed by a market downturn.

The platforms also allow you to dial up or down (usually within ranges) on your own score. Some also enable you to add different investments to customize and thus alter the risk profile of their designed portfolios, even if your score doesn't change. Our approach is: stick to the automated portfolio as closely as possible. It's formulated to give you the best chance of reaching your financial goals with the least amount of risk.

Robo investment platforms' tools to help determine your risk tolerance and manage your desire to notch it up are fairly blunt-edged instruments, but they seem reasonably effective.* The growth in robo investment platforms assets over time—even through down markets—is solid evidence that most investors are sticking to their strategies. The platforms have done a great service by helping everyday investors invest in diversified portfolios *and* stay the course. That kind of investment wisdom used to be the purview of wealthy people with traditional investment advisors, who jumped on the phone to remind investors not to sell.

How to Work with Robo Investment Platforms

You should set your risk tolerance—or adjust your portfolio—on a robo investment platform based on the answer to a deceptively simple question, stated here two

---

* If there's a definitive study on this, we haven't found it.

different ways: How much money can you afford to lose when you most need it? How much excess cash do you have?

If you have $100,000 invested, and $50,000 in cash, and the market drops $30,000 (30% loss), and you have a big emergency expense of $75,000, then you have overestimated your risk tolerance. You'll be forced to sell some of your investments at a 30% loss to cover the expense. If you had $100,000 invested and you have an emergency expense of $75,000 or you are already retired and drawing money out at a rate of $7,000 a month (so you have enough after the 30% loss to last for only 10 months), you have *seriously* overestimated your risk tolerance.

Excess cash =

Your emergency savings + 50% of your investment portfolio

If your excess cash is enough to carry you through for a few years—for instance, you lose the ability to work and have no disability insurance—then you can afford a high risk tolerance on your entire portfolio (remember, in the worst bear market in history, stocks fell 50%).

The question of how much you can afford to lose when you most need it is harder to answer than it seems. Most people could make some sacrifices rather than pull the

$75,000 out of their investment portfolio. You could go back to work. Do you need a house upgrade? Can you put off a new HVAC system for three or four years? Maybe your child's college tuition can be covered by loans. Can he or she get a part-time job? After you have enough to feed your family and keep a roof over your head, the definition of "afford" has to do with how unhappy a lack of money makes you and how much happiness money adds to your life. If you start to apply System 1, your intuitive mind, the one that takes pleasure in the day-to-day, and System 2, your rational mind, to the relationship between happiness and money, you'll be able to start to think about risk—and your risk tolerance—in a clearer way.

Consider one elderly New York City couple. They weren't wildly wealthy but were remarkably un-stressed about money. They were spending more than what was advisable in their later years, banking on the idea that they were probably going to die sooner than the longest-term life span projection. They were prepared for the worst-case scenario: running out of money and having to sell their home. "We started out eating hot dogs in one room in the Bronx," the wife of the couple said when asked about their decision to overspend. "The thought of hot dogs again doesn't bother us at all."

Were they fooling themselves? Maybe. But they had thought the decision through and had actual experience with the worst-case scenario.

The Cost of Money

Psychologists have long studied the relationship between money and happiness. A 2022 study by Matthew A. Killingsworth, Daniel Kahneman, and Barbara Mellers paints a nuanced picture.[2] For the majority of people, happiness grows with money, or more money buys more happiness, with an annual income up to $500,000. That level, $500,000, is cited as a ceiling because people earning more than that are very rare in the study's sample. But for a minority of people, about 15% in the sample, their happiness plateaus at $100,000 income. You might be in the minority, for whom making more than $100,000 income creates diminishing returns in happiness. The researchers theorized that the people in that 15% bucket have problems in their lives that can't be solved with money. (Or maybe they have simple tastes, like hot dogs.)

If you are in the majority, then making more money—up to $500,000—will likely make you happier. But you need to be realistic about your chances of getting there. An opportunity to make $150,000 or $200,000 a year doesn't come often or easily and might not be in your control at all. If that's the case, you might be better off juicing your happiness by acting on what you can control, such as being part of a community or having hobbies.

What the researchers can't say is how much of people's reported happiness comes from their assessment of what money gives them—for example "status"—and how much it comes from their lived experiences and memories of joyful events. Another way to juice your happiness may be to let go of the need for status and seek out more joy. How do you approach the question of happiness in general? How much do you value your day-to-day happiness, the experience of pleasure and pain in each day in your life (System 1) versus what researchers call your life satisfaction, which has to do with how your thinking mind assesses your happiness?

Once you have an idea of the extent to which money can make you happy and your capacity for making money, consider money and happiness from *other* directions. In the worst-case scenario, what is the least amount of money you need to feel secure, and how, from that amount of income or wealth, can you build happiness via means other than money?

Identify Your Values

The question of happiness, life satisfaction, and status are also closely related to your values. How important is it to you that you "win" in a particular career or that you have the biggest house or the best car? How big a house would you consider comfortable? How many vacations per year would make you "happy"? How nice a car would you consider an "enjoyable driving experience"? Would you send your daughter to an Ivy

League university with $60,000 annual tuition or a public state university with $8,000 annual tuition if she is accepted by both?[†] How much money do you want to donate or leave to causes after your death? These are hard questions to answer, and there are no right or wrong answers. They depend on your values.

Knowing yourself is the most important key to making good financial decisions, which in turn is the most important key to using the powerful tools on a robo investment platform in an ideal way. You'll know how hard you need to work in your job and perhaps be more prepared if at first you don't succeed. If you have judged time with your family to be more important than wealth, you might find it easier to bear when you prioritize vacations and new cars over saving for retirement. If you understand the goal you climb toward, and why, it's easier to work hard toward the goal. You'll know how much excess cash you have, so that you can invest at the highest risk level you can tolerate and not withdraw during a downturn.

You'll understand what your spending should look like, which in turn will tell you how big your emergency fund should be. You'll know whether you need a Roth IRA in addition to your traditional or SEP IRAs because you're

---

[†] Actually, a public university with $8,000 tuition is mostly a pipe dream these days.

saving for a house or graduate school. And you'll feel equipped for harder questions. We've placed a big emphasis on staying the course. But there are times when withdrawing money, even in a downturn, or at the cost of a tax penalty, is the right choice.

Will this always work out for the best? No. You can still make misjudgments. You could discover that you're utterly miserable eating hot dogs at the age of 90 and feel a mighty sense of regret. But you can live with a less-than-perfect outcome if you went into it with your eyes wide open.

There Are All Kinds of Risks

We've talked a lot about investment risk, which we defined as volatility. If you invest in the stock market, there is a risk that you will lose money in the short term and that your money won't be there when you need it.

There is another risk in taking this long-term approach to saving and investing, besides the loss of money. What if you don't live long enough to enjoy the fruits of your labor? Learning to live with this risk is part of being human. It's an individual question, but we can help you think through how it might pertain to your finances. Consider how four different people would act in one scenario.

What if you find out when you're 50 that you are going to inherit $250,000 in your later years from one of your parents, who is still living but is 35 years older than you are? In this scenario, one kind of person, Person A, might decide to relax in their career but take a higher level of risk in their portfolio because they think the $250,000 will cover their retirement expenses for five extra years, giving their portfolio more time to recover from a downturn. This is the approach that statistically speaking is the most likely to yield the most wealth and the least stress from day-to-day work. But they're facing two kinds of risk: that the inheritance won't arrive and that the market will drop.

Person B might look at this scenario and go exactly the opposite route. They might figure, reasonably, on the $250,000 arriving by the time they're 80, replacing their own retirement savings. So they could invest in dividend stocks and bonds, very safe investments, to see them through until the age of 80. They wouldn't feel the need to take a risk at all with their retirement savings. This is the approach that yields the most peace of mind. Person B doesn't have to worry about the risk in the market but is still taking a risk that the $250,000 doesn't arrive for some reason, in which case they'd be short of retirement savings.

A third person, Person C, would decide to ignore the inheritance entirely (nothing in life is guaranteed, after all). They work an extra job to make sure they have enough savings to last them through the age of 100. They're taking a risk, too. If they die young, they might never get a chance to enjoy their wealth, and they would have squandered the gift of time the inheritance might have given them. In their later years, many people regret the amount of time they spent working. This person's second risk is loss of time—which we can't quantify but is certainly painful.

A fourth person, Person D, might decide to upgrade their current life quality a little bit. They work, save, and invest. They also realize that life is short. They occasionally contemplate the possibility of their death in a car accident. They might decide to spend a portion of the $250,000 on a kitchen renovation or a Porsche they've been longing for, making a reasonable guess they will have enough money to support themselves in retirement but still taking some risk that they won't have enough.

There is no right answer here. The four people all make reasonable choices consistent with their values. A robo investment platform is safe, innovative, and flexible to help any one of these people achieve their goals. Our message in this book is that you'll be happy and successful on the platform if you know your own relationship with money and your own values. You'll be able to look back from your 80s, 90s, and 100s with fewer regrets.

Answer these questions to help understand your attitude toward risk:

1. How much excess cash do you have?
2. How much are you able to lose in your investment portfolio if the loss comes at the worst possible time (remembering that the market historically has always rebounded but can take a few years)? Will you still have enough to retire if the worst-case loss happens around retirement age?
3. What is the least amount of income you could get by on and still be happy?
4. How much happier would you be if you made a lot more money?
5. What would you do if you learned that you might get a $250,000 inheritance?

Key Takeaways in This Chapter

1. Robo investment platforms help you identify your risk tolerance, which is based on your ability to financially sustain a loss at the worst possible time in your life.
2. If the risk tolerance level on the platform is higher than it should be, you're at risk for panicking when there's a downturn or running short of cash—or both.
3. The biggest mistake investors make is cashing out when the market turns down.

4. Thinking through how much excess cash you have is more complicated than it seems. One formula is your emergency savings + 50% of your investment portfolio.
5. Your attitude toward money may increase or decrease your risk tolerance.
6. There are other kinds of risk, including the risk of trading too much of your time for money.

Chapter Twelve

Live for the Present, Invest for the Future

~

Lounging on a gray sofa in her living room, with white calla lilies on a glass coffee table beside her, Qian managed to write a few paragraphs in the *Little Book of Robo Investing*. She wanted to write more but struggled over thinking of intuitive examples to illustrate abstract investing concepts. Her brain was fried. She worked from 8:30 a.m. to 6:30 p.m. at her full-time corporate job, drove home, went for a three-mile run before sunset, grabbed a quick bite, took a shower, and wrote for two hours. It was 10 p.m. The day felt productive and mentally exhausting. She noticed a bottle of Glenlivet in a corner, with a last sip of golden whiskey left at the bottom. A full day of very hard work and a three-mile run justified a sip and a moment of relaxation, she concluded. She poured the last sip over ice cubes.

Qian spends most of her waking hours on activities that produce delayed gratification—a full-time job, a part-time writing project, eating healthy, and exercise. When you are in the midst of these activities, you experience mostly challenges and almost no enjoyment. You don't see results either, not immediately, not after days or weeks. The benefit created in a day is so tiny that it is basically nonexistent. Nevertheless, without you realizing, the tiny daily benefit accumulates and evolves into something remarkable. After a long time, months, years, or even decades, Qian will be rewarded with a good career and secure financial life.

To become a great investor, you must also consider the value and transformative power of time. Like risk and goals, the value of time is personal. That leads us to a funny misconception about investing, one of the final ones we're going to discuss:

Misconception #14: Investing is all about money.

The truth is that investing is also about time, because time acts so powerfully upon money to help us reach our goals (or to keep us from reaching them). Though we've touched on time in other chapters in this book, it's so important that we want to give it its own chapter here, toward the end.

First, we're going to talk about the need for balance and then offer a section about specific cases in which time is a surprisingly powerful force, one to be approached with care and with your calculator or ChatGPT at hand.

The Key Is Balance

On a robo investing platform, the approach to making money is balance. You balance your budget to have money to invest, and the robo investment platform balances your portfolio to help you make money in your sleep. This philosophy also extends to the way you spend your time.

It is hard and unsustainable for us to spend 100% of our waking hours on challenging activities through solely motivating ourselves with the delayed gratification that would be produced in the future. Even if we are so disciplined that we can live our lives this way, we would be forever living in the future and miss the beauty of the present: the calla lilies and the sip of whiskey.

In addition to investing small amounts regularly over time in your portfolio, we suggest allocating small amounts of your money regularly to the present day. We need instant gratification—indulgence, relaxation, and fun sprinkled here and there, to live a satisfying life short-term and long-term. For Qian it's a sip of whiskey after a long stretch of work. For Elizabeth it's a Montana summer day with her children, Lillie and Quinn. Because she is self-employed, time off has a real financial cost.

Your ability to balance the present and the future shapes your approach to money. For some people, it's all about instant gratification with no consideration of the future. They spend all their monthly income on life necessities *and* luxuries. They buy expensive toys or vacations they can't afford by maxing out credit cards and carrying balances at a horrifying 25% interest rate. They don't save. Investing is an even more remote concept. They live in the moment 24/7 as if the future of having to pay down massive credit card debts and support themselves financially in retirement would never come. The instant gratification extreme is not uncommon in the consumeristic society in the United States, where about 40% of the adults can't cover a $400 unexpected expense, according to a 2022 survey by the Federal Reserve.[1]

For other people the pendulum swings to another extreme. It's all about delayed gratification with life pleasures forbidden. They are extreme versions of *frugal millionaires.* They work all the time, to save as much as possible. They live in the smallest apartment, cook the cheapest ingredients at home, buy second-hand clothes at thrift stores, never take family vacations, and buy few holiday gifts. They strategize how much more they can save for the future by deprioritizing the present. They are able to save a significant portion of their monthly income and become millionaires over a long period of time. They also experience satisfaction, or at least they don't mind, during the process; otherwise they wouldn't be able to stick to their financial philosophy long enough to become millionaires.

If You Have the Wherewithal to Be a Frugal Millionaire, Go for It

We celebrate the extreme frugal millionaires for finding a system that rewards them, financially and psychologically. If the system resonates with you, give it a try. We don't advocate it, however, because it isn't a satisfying life for most people. Saving and investing are important. Your money grows over time so you can consume in the future: big-ticket items such as a down payment for a house, college tuition for your kids or a dream Caribbean family vacation, or recurring small-ticket items such as groceries and utility bills when you retire. You should also consume today to enjoy your present life, within your means: an overpriced smoothie at Jamba Juice after a hike in the heat, a red lipstick to cheer yourself up after a heartbreaking breakup, a new bike after you've had a setback in your career, a restaurant dinner to celebrate a milestone, a new car or kitchen renovation when you have a big windfall and you have money left over after accounting reasonably for your long-term needs. The present consumption costs money and would make you save less for the future, but the peace, satisfaction, happiness, and bonding "bought" with money at important moments of life are priceless.

Life is about the present. Investing is about the future. This book is about investing, but we do not suggest you forgo 100% of instant gratification at the present for the benefit of delayed gratification in the future. To prepare for the future, make sure you live below your means and save and invest an amount every month sufficient to fund your and your family's future financial needs. Adjust those financial needs down, if needed. To live in the present, consume things or experiences that bring you and your loved ones happiness and you can comfortably afford.

Develop a Healthy Respect for the Power of Time

We advised in the early chapters of this book that the philosophy of robo investment platforms is to make time your ally. To extend that allyship into your life, understand and respect it. Here are three specific cases where time is a surprisingly powerful variable in investing. The only way to get a handle on it is to employ your System-2 mind, and do the math on the specific scenario that you are facing. We want to get you thinking about how to thoughtfully incorporate time into your financial decision-making.

1. Compounding

One big difference between the wealthy and people who don't have a lot of money is that wealthy people enjoy a feeling of financial security. Those who don't have enough—however they define enough—spend time worrying about paying this bill, or that bill, a drain that is constant and depleting.

Time can be the great equalizer in delivering that invaluable sense of financial security because of the power of compounding. Remember the quick-and-dirty rule that your portfolio will double in size every 10 years. If you invest even small amounts every month, say $50 in your late teens and early 20s, $200–500 when you are employed, with contributions increasing as you need to make up shortfalls for the goals you set, you will end with a portfolio valued in the millions. You won't be Elon Musk. But you'll have the same sense he likely does of having what you need.

2. Debt

Your debt payments grow over time, just like your portfolio compounds. If you borrow $300,000 for a house, with a 7% interest rate, you will pay

$418,000 in interest, plus your principal, for a total of $718,000. What this means is simple: be very careful about borrowing money, because you're often paying more than you realize over time for the privilege. In the case of a loan for a house, apply a Depression-era piece of old wisdom: it's OK to borrow for an asset that appreciates in value. Given the tax break on interest on your home mortgage, the fact that you need to pay for a roof over your head whether as a renter or buyer, and that you can tap your home equity in retirement, a house is one of the best investments for Americans.

Our opinion on other kinds of debt: Education loans are a toss-up; they may be worthwhile if you are significantly increasing your earning potential. The hard-and-fast rule on credit card debt is simple: don't use it if you can possibly avoid it. A $10,000 debt at 24% annual interest rate will take you seven years to pay off, if you make payments of $250 a month; at the end of the term, you will have paid a total of more than $20,319. Pay off the balance every month. But don't beat yourself up if you have some debt! The financial services industry is expert at marketing credit cards. If you have high-interest-rate credit card debt, paying it off becomes one of your top priorities.

3. Inflation

Specific predictions made by humans are very apt to be wrong, but most experts agree as of the writing of this book, 2023, that inflation is likely to be between 2% and 5% for the next few years. In general, an inflationary environment means you should save and invest even more than you think you'll need, because you will need to withdraw more money to maintain your living standards. Assume you have a $1 million retirement portfolio that earns 5% return per year after tax. You withdraw $50,000 in your first year of retirement and increase the amount by the inflation rate every year. If the inflation rate is 2%, your portfolio will last for 30 years. If the inflation rate is higher, for example, 5%, you will withdraw more to pay for higher living expenses and unfortunately your portfolio will only last for 20 years. That makes it imperative to invest, because investing in a diversified portfolio has been shown over time to beat inflation. A 7% rate of return minus 5% inflation is still 2%.

Inflation (and the power of time) has another, hidden effect, one that can be beneficial for long-term borrowers. If the interest rate on your long-term debt is lower than the rate of inflation, time is once again your ally: when you're paying off the money over 20 or 30 years, you're paying it off with money that is worth less.

Keeping It Real

Qian loves to surf, and Elizabeth loves to do yoga. Both require balance. The past three years have felt like trying to surf or do yoga in a hurricane. How could anyone have kept their balance? We all navigated Covid—the massive confusion, disruption to everyday life, social isolation, and chaotic rollout of vaccines. Some of us contracted Covid. Some of us lost people we loved. The political landscape in America features impeachments and criminal investigations of a former president, protests against police brutality, mass shootings, and the Supreme Court's decision to overturn *Roe v. Wade*. Extreme weather rolled over our planet, in fires, hurricanes, and droughts. As many as four in ten US adults (41%) experienced high levels of psychological distress at least once between March 2020 and September 2022, according to the Pew Research Center.[2] Women, youth, disabled, lower-income workers, and solo dwellers had even a higher share of distress. The pandemic was only one of the stressors—economic uncertainty and worries about the nation's future also hurt Americans' mental health.

In an environment such as this, it's doubly hard to engage your rational mind, to delay gratification, or do the calculations that help you make wise judgments about budgeting, money, and investing. Even your System-2 mind, looking at the last three years, might throw in the towel and decide that a rational choice was to give up on the future and live entirely for the present. But tumultuous times do not change the basic processes about how to build financial security. Everybody needs to calibrate for both the chaotic present and the unknown future.

Control What You Can Control

The market is an imperfect mirror of the macro environment, our world. The world and the market are volatile, unpredictable, and out of your control. If you let your environment dictate your feelings and decisions, you surrender your life to randomness. Instead, live your life intentionally and focus on what you can control. When it comes to investing, you can control a few levers. Find a fiduciary platform so you're in a safe space. Invest for the long run, diversify broadly, use low-fee investments, use tax-efficient investments, and stick to a proven strategy. Look for the balanced approach, in investing and in the way you spend your time and money.

We don't have answers for the enormous questions of our times. But one simple and effective way to cope with distress is to take concrete actions. Get up and go outside, reach out to a friend, volunteer with a community group, get some exercise. We humbly suggest another small concrete action in the face of uncertainty is to keep investing.

Key Takeaways in This Chapter

1. Investing is about money and time.

2. When you are making financial decisions, factor in the value of time, including when it comes to compounding, debt, and inflation.

3. Delaying gratification pays off, but most people shouldn't go to the extreme. Budget time and money for joy in the present, as well as value in the future.

4. Tumultuous times make it harder—but more important—to maintain a balanced approach.

Winning Strategy for Volatile Times

Uncertainty in the macro environment usually translates into volatility in the markets. That has been true in the past few years. In 2020, the market dropped sharply and rebounded somewhat thereafter. In 2021, we had a large sustained gain. In 2022, the market became a bear market. In 2023, the bear market continued for the first part of the year.

In Section 2 of this book, we talked about robo investment platforms' ability to take over many of the painful-yet-important activities, such as rebalancing and tax-loss harvesting, for a lower fee. But there is something you can do, as well, beyond staying the course. However, it requires letting go of another misconception:

Misconception #15: Volatile times are a bad time to invest.

Today's uncertainty, and therefore volatility, may continue in the short term and will certainly return at some point in the long term. Continuing to invest through these conditions keeps you from making investors' biggest mistake, trying to time the market and therefore missing the one-day upswings. And it also turns out that volatility, though unpleasant to live through, can be good for your portfolio. Once again, the key to doing well in uncertain times and volatile market is balance.

When volatility increases, it's tempting to stop investing and pull your money out of the market to avoid the whipsaw feeling and the fear of loss if you dwell on it. Some people might have another instinct: pour lots of money into risky investments, trying to build up enough wealth to feel secure.

But as the chart produced by Burt Malkiel a few years ago shows, volatile markets are actually good times to invest, if—this is important—you're keeping up with a regular schedule of investing.[3] Investing regularly in small amounts over time is called dollar cost averaging. In a volatile market, you can buy more shares of an index fund at a lower cost. That gives you the chance to benefit more when shares increase.

(*Continued*)

The Effects of Dollar Cost Averaging

		VOLATILE FLAT MARKET		RISING MARKET	
Period	Amount Invested	Price of Index Fund	# of Shares Purchased	Price of Index Fund	# of Shares Purchased
1	$1,000	$100	10	$100	10
2	$1,000	$75	13.33	$110	9.09
3	$1,000	$55	18.18	$120	8.33
4	$1,000	$110	9.09	$130	7.69
5	$1,000	$100	10	$140	7.14
Total	**$5,000**		**60.60**		**42.25**
Average Cost of Shares Purchased			**$82.51**		**$118.34**
Value at Period 5			**$6,060**		**$5,915**

$$Average\ cost\ of\ shares\ purchased = \frac{Amount\ Invested}{Total\ shares\ purchased}$$

$$Value\ at\ Period\ 5 = Total\ shares\ purchased \times Price\ of\ Index\ Fund\ (Period\ 5)$$

Source: Burton Malkiel / https://www.wealthfront.com/blog/wp-content/uploads/2015/08/DCA-chart.png / Wealthfront Corporation.

Section Four

Where You Begin

Chapter Thirteen

Is a Robo Investment Platform Right for You?

~

Surgeons apply best practices to treating your body, based on hundreds of years of research and evidence, to give you the best chance of recovery. You wouldn't do surgery yourself, but you'd also shop around to find the best surgeon. A good robo investment platform is like a surgeon.

We rely on professional help for most of the important things in our lives, and we seek regular checkups and aid for problems and emergencies. Surgeons make our bodies better. HVAC experts keep us cool or warm. Car mechanics help us go. God forbid the vet isn't there when our dog is sick!*

Yet, many people don't realize they could benefit from professional help with their investments. It's hard to know what you're not seeing, so in this chapter, we're going to summarize the benefits of professional, **low-priced** help.

But you might be an investor just starting out, unsure of the value of investment advice, or someone who thinks they don't need investment help at all.

Misconception #16: A Do-It-Yourself investment strategy is just as good as a robo investment platform.

If you are trying to invest on your own, you're almost certainly making less money than you could be, taking on too much risk, and spending too much time doing it. If you're not investing at all because you're worried about fees, you're at a serious risk of not being able to retire securely or meet your other financial goals. Ten years ago, before the advent of low-cost robo investment platforms, it was a lot harder to make a great return because the fees were eating into people's returns. That's not the case today.

---

*OK, fine. Or cat.

But still, people don't seek help from a robo investment platform for five reasons:

1. They don't know what's available today and how it would benefit them.
2. They think all investment advice is overpriced, and they've been burned in the past.
3. They think they can do just as well or better investing on their own.
4. They have an emotional hang-up, such as procrastination or lack of trust.
5. They really can't or shouldn't use one.

Let's look at them one at a time.

1. What's Available Today, and How Will It Benefit Me?

Most people, from investors just starting out to frugal millionaires, can benefit greatly from the approach to investing that we've outlined in this book. They need to invest to beat inflation, retire with financial security, and meet their other financial goals. But many people haven't sought out this approach, because they don't know it exists or that it would work for them.

In Chapter 1, we explained that investing today is about investing in low-cost index funds that represent different asset classes and sticking to your plan over decades. This approach is based on investing research of the last 50 years. In Chapters 2–7, we explained how robo investment platforms implement Nobel Prize–winning research and behavioral science. Robo investing is the best and most convenient way of capturing the overall returns of the markets, which have produced solid returns for the past 50 years, while at the same time de-risking your portfolio. You can't remove the risk from investing. But if you plan well and diversify properly, you can lessen the risk and be reasonably sure you'll have enough money for your needs, even in an extended market downturn.

Robo investing is revolutionary because it lowered the price of this high-quality approach to investment, making it accessible to everyone. The platforms offer a collection of different kinds of accounts on one easy-to-access interface, including tax-deferred retirement accounts, insured high-yield cash accounts, and taxable investment accounts for medium-term goals such as buying a house. It's easy to keep track of your financial life because of this holistic view of your finances. And because the platforms are fiduciaries, they are likely to roll out high-quality innovations over time.

2. Are Robo Investment Platforms Overpriced? Compared to What?

Some people don't seek out professional investment advice because they think it's for rich people, not for them. And it's true that investment advice has been very costly in the past. Traditional investment advisors often charge 1% of the value of your portfolio to manage your investments, and they make money from commissions on high-priced mutual funds and other fees. Brokers, who trade stocks and bonds and sometimes offer investment advice on the side, particularly have a bad reputation for taking advantage of investors.

In our 20s, neither of us could afford high-priced investment advice from traditional fiduciary financial advisors, which was all that was available at the time. It wasn't just the high fee; it was the account minimum of $500,000. Luckily, both of us were good at saving. But in retrospect, we look back at that time and wonder how much we gave away in returns by investing only through workplace retirement plans and by haphazard, short-term approaches to investing on our own.

There were no other options for people like us who weren't already wealthy. But this picture changed 10 years ago, with robo investment platforms. Robo investment advisors are like the car industry after Henry Ford figured out how to build an assembly line.

These days, it's possible to find high-quality investment advice for less than 0.35% of your total assets under management per year. (Those are the fees for the investment platform service—fees for the funds or for access to human advisors add to the total.) We think this is a fair price for everything that you get from a robo investment platform, and we like the transparency of many of the platforms about their fees.

3. Can DIY Investors Really Do Just as Well Investing on Their Own? Science Says No

You might still be reluctant to pay the low cost of a robo investment platform, and we get that. We both have a horror of financial fees, because we know how much they add up over time. But we also know it's impossible for a DIY investor to do some of what science tells us is the best way to plan, earn returns, and manage risks. DIY investors aren't capable of best-in-class diversification, disciplined rebalancing, and tax-loss harvesting. We believe the low fee for this level of investment service is worth it.[†]

You can decide not to believe the science that shows that it's impossible to beat the market consistently, which

---

[†] Wealthfront has released data showing that tax-loss harvesting tax savings made up for fees for investors with taxable accounts.

we wrote about in detail in Section 2 of this book. You can decide you don't trust professionals, even the low-cost, highly regulated ones. Some people are really stubborn, and for some people, the stubborn approach generally works. In investing, it really doesn't work. If you're a DIY investor, you are likely allowing your System-1 mind to overcome your System-2 mind. (We talked about the science of behavioral finance in Chapter 8.)

This strain of rugged individualism is deeply baked into the American psyche. Have you ever seen the movie *The Revenant?* In the movie, based on the true story of a frontiersman Hugh Glass in 1823, the main character is mauled by a grizzly bear and abandoned by his companions. In a particularly gruesome scene, Hugh, as played by Leonardo DiCaprio, cauterizes a wound in his own neck after he attempts to drink water that leaks from the throat wound. Perhaps you want to be the investment version of Hugh Glass, fighting the bears and making your own way across the wilderness, cauterizing your own neck if need be. In that case, trading apps and stock buying might be for you. Go for it. You be you.[‡]

[‡] Amy Tikkanen, "Hugh Glass Frontiersman," in *Encyclopedia Britannica*, August 11, 2023, https://www.britannica.com/biography/Hugh-Glass. You might be interested in the end of Hugh Glass's story: He made it 200 miles to Fort Kiowa, where he recuperated. He apparently survived in part because of his determination to kill his two companions. But history

If we sound frustrated, that is because of the people who have approached us at cocktail parties or work events to ask why the fast-growth ETF that holds shares in innovative energy companies they bought last year took a dive[§] or who are angry because AT&T's stock dropped in the wake of a news report.[**] "Why did these things happen?" is not the right question. Why you bought a single stock or risky ETF thinking you could beat the collective wisdom of the public stock market *is*.

4. Can You Overcome the Emotional Hang-Ups?

There are people who, for various emotional reasons, haven't started investing. They know they ought to invest, but they're not sure how or they're reluctant to start. They don't have the confidence in themselves to be able to evaluate the service they're getting in exchange for the fee charged. We understand completely! Commitments are hard. For these

---

(not the movie) reports that when he eventually caught up with them, his anger had dissipated. He forgave one, who had only been 19 at the time of the incident, and either forgave or gave up looking for the other. There's a lesson in there for DIYers. Just keep in mind that the ideas that drove you in the past, such as independence, might not be the same ideas that will serve you in the future.

[§] Conversation with Johns Hopkins University student and Army officer, Aug. 24, 2023, Washington, DC.

[**] Conversation with self-made millionaire, July 15, 2023, Polson, MT.

investors, robo investment platforms are a great place to start because they are straightforward and account minimums are relatively low, $0–5,000.

Maybe you'll recognize yourself in one of the following emotional traps. Many people we know have been in more than one.

I Can't Save! They know they ought to be investing every month, and have the room in their budgets. (We talk about budgeting in Chapter 10.) But the idea of setting aside hundreds of dollars every month from the free spending is hard. We've been there. Start small, even as small as an automatic deduction of $100 or $200 a month into your emergency savings (first) or your retirement account. You'll see how fast and painlessly your total builds up and be motivated to keep going. The key is to make the deduction automatic. Remember that you can turn off the deduction at any point if you need to. But we bet that after three months, you won't even think about it anymore.

Stubborn Independence. They're already investing with a brokerage without much support. Unlike DIYers, they don't take any real joy in investing on their own; they just do it because they don't want to pay any fee at all to an investment advisor and think they'll do fine with a collection of mutual funds and index funds. They're probably doing OK, but they are giving up a point or two each year in their returns, and they may be anxious about their money because they don't have ready and immediate access to information about their whole financial lives.

Never Starting. Some people are scared of investing or lack the confidence to take the first step. Many keep too much locked up in CDs, cash, or US Treasury bonds (these can be defined as a form of low-volatility investing). Some don't recognize they face the risk of inflation. Some lack the financial planning tools to figure out how much cash they need. They worry they will make a mistake on a robo investment platform. If you're in this category, please read the first section of this book to understand why this scientific approach to investing is safe enough and why you can't afford not investing.

Support Seeking. Some people want a relationship with a traditional financial advisor. They want someone who knows the names of their dog and their children, and they're willing to pay—not for better investment advice but for emotional support.

Too Busy. Some people are not comfortable using even the simple robo investment websites and apps. They don't want to follow a short learning curve. If you're one of these, open an account at one of the robo investment advisors we list in Chapter 14. Fund it with a small amount of money. If it feels comfortable and trustworthy, add to it over time.

Two Categories of Investors Who Shouldn't Be on a Robo Investment Platform

Die-Hard DIYers. Some people just really love stock trading, owning individual stocks, or buying investments they're excited about. Discount or free brokerages from E*Trade to Robinhood have made that easier and cheaper, probably to the long-term detriment of most investors. The evidence shows this kind of investing underperforms automated investing strategies, such as the ones on the robo investment platforms, over time. The general upward direction of the market can mean that you could see healthy returns in your portfolio over time no matter how haphazardly you invest, and the emotional satisfaction might make up for any underperformance compared with a research-driven approach.

But please, don't take too much risk. Don't bet more than you can afford on a few stocks or new investment schemes. This is serious business: In 2020, a 20-year-old trader killed himself after he thought he'd lost more than $700,000 trading options on Robinhood.[1] The company settled a lawsuit by his family without admitting wrongdoing.

Complex Clients. Some people truly have a complicated financial life, perhaps because they have very large quantities of assets, more than $5 million. If you want to set up a trust, invest in hedge funds or through private equity firms, or need to manage a large estate, it is likely more convenient to use a traditional advisor who is willing to charge less than 1% per year on your portfolio.

If you identify with some of these characters, ask yourself the following questions. If you answer "no" or "I don't know" to many, you could use the low-cost investment advice and the holistic financial view of a robo investment platform.

1. Do I have financial goals, and am I saving and investing to meet them?
2. How is my current investment portfolio, including retirement funds, doing relative to the appropriate benchmark? If I am mainly invested in stocks, is my portfolio matching the performance of the S&P 500 over time? If I have a mix of asset classes, am I doing better or worse than a 60/40 portfolio of stocks and bonds? (We will talk about appropriate benchmarks in Chapter 14).
3. Is my portfolio outperforming inflation?
4. Is my financial situation—including my job, my family support, and my cash savings—stable enough to last through a major bear market of two or three years so I didn't need to sell at a loss?
5. How much do I enjoy stock trading? Is this a good use of my time?

6. Do I trust professionals to help with my financial life?
7. Can I afford the high fees of a human financial advisor, who might be standing in for a therapist, but charging me way too much for the emotional support?

You Can't See What You Don't Know

When Elizabeth was eight years old, she went to the eye doctor for the first time, a visit prompted by a poor vision test at school. The doctor prescribed glasses. The moment she put the glasses on, she could see the individual leaves on trees, visible for the first time at a distance. It was a revelatory moment, so powerful she remembers it to this day.

Understanding that there is a straightforward research-based approach to investing, available on low-cost robo investment platforms, feels like a revelation to many people.

Robo investment platforms work best for those who need the higher returns of the stock market, who have the critical thinking skills to set their own goals, and who don't want to spend a ton of time thinking about their investments. That includes almost everyone.. But not all robo investment platforms are the same. In the next chapter, we'll talk about how to pick the right one for you.

Key Takeaways in This Chapter

1. Most investors benefit from the low-cost, high-quality advice on robo investment platforms.

2. Scientifically based investment advice is another kind of professional service, like that provided by doctors.

3. A few types of people shouldn't use robo investment platforms, including those who love trading so much they are willing to risk underperforming and those who have very complex financial situations.

4. Some people allow their emotions—usually fear—to keep them from investing with a robo advisor, or in some cases from investing at all. Don't be one of them.

Chapter Fourteen

Find the Right Platform

～

Picking a robo investment platform is like shopping for a combination of a smartphone and your doctor. You want the right features for you, packaged in the convenience and shine of a nifty tech platform. But you also want a platform that works well and is run by people who are ethical and thoughtful, even if you interact with them directly only rarely. And you want the company to be transparent in its practices and to be regulated so you have peace of mind.

Misconception #17: It's impossible to pick between robo investment platforms.

The first thing to decide, or be relatively certain of, is your investment approach. We hope that in this book we convinced you to live below your means and to invest small amounts regularly in long-term, low-fee, tax-smart investments. Once you've committed to that strategy, you can go about deciding on the robo investment advisor that's right for you.

This chapter is divided into three sections:

1. List of robo investment platforms as of summer 2023 and some things to keep in mind when evaluating them;
2. Features of the platforms; and
3. How to check up on your robo investment platform (or other investment approaches).

Comparing Robo Investment Platforms

Here's a list of 13 prominent robo investment platforms, in alphabetical order. These are stand-alone companies or owned by larger investment firms. Because the industry is evolving rapidly, we're not going to write specifically about the features of individual companies but rather, try to give you the tools to evaluate them. The financial media often releases comparisons of robo investment advisors, but investors should be wary of relying too extensively on any one of the lists. Because robo investment platforms can pay to be ranked, many lists are somewhat biased, especially against new and innovative players.

Robo Investment Platforms*

Acorns
Axos Invest
Betterment
Ellevest
Fidelity Go
Future Advisor by Blackrock
JP Morgan Automated Investing
Schwab Intelligent Portfolios
SigFig
SoFi Wealth
US Bancorp Automated Investor
Vanguard Digital Advisor
Wealthfront
Wells Fargo Intuitive Investor

---

*These companies have some features of robo investment platforms or are newcomers that might develop more services: Ally Invest, Blooom, Citi Wealth Builder, E*Trade Core Portfolios, M1 Finance, Marcus Invest, Merrill Guided Investing, Titan, UBS Advice Advantage.

All these platforms share the basic approach of diversifying over multiple asset classes and using index funds to invest in asset classes. They also generally have low platform fees. Beyond that, there are different flavors. For example, Betterment provides human advisors for larger accounts; Vanguard Digital Advisor only uses Vanguard's own index funds, generally considered best in class; Ellevest is designed to be female friendly; and Wealthfront remains the most tech-forward.

To pick a platform, we suggest four steps:

1. Ask around. Just as when you are shopping for a doctor, your friends and neighbors are good sources of information. Ask them which platforms they use and what they like versus do not like about the platforms. The downside is that they may not be experts. The upside is that they will be unbiased.

2. Research online. Some of the sources of information are biased, but reading two or three articles from a variety of sources will ground you in the most common features offered by the different platforms. As of this writing, two big differentiators in the industry were the platforms that offer tax-loss harvesting and the platforms that offer access to a human advisor, usually for larger accounts. Online resources often provide each platform's assets under management and number

of accounts to indicate its size. You can prioritize larger and more established platforms if you feel safety in numbers.

3. Research enforcement actions against the companies at the SEC and FINRA, at sec.gov or at BrokerCheck .com. In the finance industry, regulatory actions are part of the normal course of business, and it's likely you'd find at least one regulatory action against every robo investment platform or company. The size of the fine tells you how seriously the SEC took the offense, and the details of what the fine was for are important, too.

4. Open a small test account on any of the platforms. The easiest way to do this (on the platforms with low minimums) is with a cash account. That will help you figure out if you like the interface. Or open a small taxable investment account, to see if you like the robo investment platform approach in general. (We wouldn't advise creating a trial retirement account. You need to keep a coherent investment strategy in your retirement accounts, and having a lot of small accounts complicates the coherency.)

Values to Keep in Mind

Financial services tends to be a sticky industry. Once you're committed to a specific platform, it's hard to change, and most people don't go to the trouble. That means you want a company whose long-term values align with yours: some combination of flexibility, integrity, transparency, and responsiveness, *plus* the features you desire. There are a handful of good indicators of a company's values, including whether the platform offers you the ability to customize portfolios and by how much; whether it offers ESG or social good investing, and how much it charges for that service; and how transparent it is about fees, in addition to how high they are.

Stock Trading or Custom Allocations

The best part about robo investing is being able to turn over the design and long-term management of your portfolios to a scientific approach. By definition, robo investment portfolios give you the best chance of the highest return for the least amount of risk. However, some robo investment platforms also offer you the ability to customize your portfolio or trade individual stocks and bonds.

We call this "playing the market." It literally is just playing; it's for fun. You might be researching companies or investment trends and want to see how well you do playing against the combined wisdom of tens of thousands of professional investors and top-notch algorithms working in the market today. You can also tweak the recommendations of robo investment platforms by changing the asset allocations your platform has given you.

Both of these are technically attempts to beat the market, and science tells us the end result of either of these activities is likely to be an underperformance of the classic portfolios over time. But if you have fun doing either one, look for a platform that offers this ability. We suggest that you limit the amount that you play with, to under 5% of your portfolio.

ESG (Environmental, Social, and Governance)

Most robo investment platforms also offer ESG portfolios or portfolios designed to exclude index funds invested in certain sectors, such as fossil fuel companies and military suppliers. The research so far suggests that these portfolios underperform, over time, index funds that are designed to mirror broad market indexes. But if your values are such that you are willing to accept a somewhat higher risk (which it's impossible to quantify because the ESG field is evolving so quickly) and, possibly, a lower performance over time, the option is there.[†] ESG portfolios usually cost more. Remember that a slightly higher fee can add up over time.

[†] It's also possible that ESG funds will deliver higher returns over time, if governments around the world begin to force companies to pay individually for collective damage, such as to the environment.

The Math on Fees

Robo investment platforms have mostly been committed to sticking to their low-cost roots. But the history of the investment industry suggests that fees creep up, even at the best-managed companies with the best-intentioned executives. Avoid platforms that have increased their fees. Here's one thing to watch out for: in some cases, the funds, the trades, and the robo investment platform are managed by the same company. Most of the time, these are large financial institutions that started offering a robo investment platform after the independent companies broke the ground. Robo platforms owned by big companies sometimes use in-house index funds, so the company has the flexibility to dial up or down the funds' expense ratios and the robo platform's fee. Sometimes the company might even provide the robo platform for "free" and only charge expenses on the funds, in which case the funds' fees are higher than similar alternatives. There are other hidden costs too, such as requiring you to keep a minimum amount in a cash account, which reduces the amount of money you have to invest in the market.

When you sign up with a robo advisor and as you're checking up on your platform, look for three fees. Total them to see how much you're really paying over time, and remember that a 1% difference is *huge* over the life of your portfolio.

1. Look for transaction fees. If you plan to trade individual stocks and bonds on your robo investment platform (which we don't think is a good idea for most people), check to see if there's a fee for trades. And look to see if the platform is charging you to deposit or withdraw money.

2. When the robo investment platform offers you a selection of funds, check their expense ratios. Look to make sure the platform is offering you funds with expense ratios under 0.15%.

3. And finally, look for the platform fee (or alternatively "advisory fee") for your portfolio, annually. It'll either be a percentage or a monthly flat fee. If it's a monthly flat fee, make sure to add up the total and see how it compares to a percentage fee. In some cases, large portfolios are charged more. A few robo investor platforms charge extra for access to human advisors.

Keep in mind that robo investment platforms are much lower cost than traditional advisors, especially a traditional advisor who is using expensive mutual funds. A comparison by NerdWallet of 10 robo investment platforms found average platform fees ranging from 0–0.35%, and a few with low monthly flat fees of under $15. A portfolio of low-cost index funds has an expense ratio of under 0.15%. Your total cost is easily under 0.5% a year.[1]

Compare that to what you'd be paying at a traditional advisor using high-cost funds. The total fees on your high-cost traditionally managed portfolio could be more than 1% a year not even including the higher fund fees. And that, as we showed you in Chapter 5, could mean a difference of more than $136,000 for a smart American saving for retirement.

Hidden Fees

In Chapter 5, we noted how fees in the finance industry are like a whack-a-mole game. You think you've knocked them down, but they pop up elsewhere. Two examples are investment platforms that charge for transactions, such as buying stocks on your behalf or transferring funds to your bank account. A $50 or $75 fee per transfer can add up fast. These don't show up in either your fund expense ratios or the advisory/platform fee. Other investment platforms may be part of fund companies and therefore steer you into their own funds, which could have higher expense ratios or transaction costs. We mentioned that earlier, but the point here is to note that it's a deceptive way of charging you more. You ought to mind both the higher fee and the deceptive way it's levied on you. These practices are common in the finance industry and have migrated into the relatively new business of robo investment platforms.

The finance industry in America is inventive, quick to copy new ideas, and quick to try to make them more profitable, sometimes at the expense of individual investors. The industry is in constant competition within itself and in a constant pull-me-pull-you relationship with the government, which protects individual investors, sometimes imperfectly. Financial services aren't free, and the people who design and run them deserve to be paid. But a good company will be transparent about fees.

Features of Robo Investment Platforms

The three pillars of quality on robo investment platforms, as we wrote in the first part of the book, are de-risking by diversification, keeping fees low, and minimizing taxes. In addition, you want a platform that helps you keep your money in the market and gives you a holistic view of your finances.

Here's a checklist of features to look for on the platforms

Fiduciary

Is the online platform you're looking at a registered investment advisor or an online brokerage? RIA is the highest standard of regulation, because RIAs are bound by a fiduciary duty to act in the best interests of their clients. Online brokerages that focus on stock trading cannot by definition be fiduciaries, because the evidence is so clear that stock trading does not make typical investors wealthy over the long term. If the robo investment platform you're checking out doesn't advertise its fiduciary status, ask.

Regulatory Standing and Assets Under Management (AUM)

How long has the platform been around? Experimenting is great if you can afford it, but we hesitate to do more than experiment with a brand-new player. In truth, the science of investing—diversification, rebalancing, tax-loss harvesting, and behavioral support—is complicated to implement in software. Some companies do it well, and others are only mediocre.

Has the platform been penalized by the federal government for treating clients badly or putting them at risk? You can turn up these fines by searching in Google or looking directly at sec.gov in the enforcement section. If you're a DIYer considering switching to a robo investment platform, you can check on enforcement actions against brokerages by looking at FINRA's BrokerCheck service.

Transparency

All robo advisors should publish the pretax returns on their different portfolios. Be wary of working with them if they don't.

Suitability

Complicated portfolios could require access to a traditional advisor who offers estate planning or high-end tax services.

Fees

Is the advisory or platform fee less than 0.3% of your portfolio? Does the platform use index funds, and are the expense ratios generally under 0.15%?

Diversification

Does the platform use index funds that represent broad swaths of the market?

Are there enough asset classes represented in the standard portfolios it offers, more than five?

Does it have a system for integrating new investment research and adding asset classes to its mix?

Taxes

Does the platform offer tax-loss harvesting?

Does it integrate with tax preparation software?

Has the SEC said anything about the quality of the company's tax-loss harvesting service?

Account Minimum

Do you have enough to open an account? Keep in mind, though, that larger account minimums are no guarantee of quality. However, you need enough to get started.

User Interface and Financial Planning

Do you like the interface, and do you find the financial planning tools easy to use and understand?
Does it help you gain a holistic view of your finances?
Does it incentivize you to save?
Does it offer a mobile app, iOS or Android, for convenience?
Does it allow you to play and stray from its portfolio designs within limits?

Some platforms will allow you to add individual stocks and new asset classes to your portfolios. Playing with your investments, within limits, can make investing more fun.

ESG Portfolio

ESG stands for environmental, social, and governance. These kinds of portfolios could underperform the market over time and tend to cost more. But some investors are willing to risk giving up some of their returns to feel more comfortable that they aren't invested in certain kinds of stocks, such as those of fossil fuel or gun companies.

Security and Privacy

Cybersecurity is an increasing concern, as is privacy, which we share. The financial services industry is regulated, which offers *some* comfort. For instance, financial services companies, including robo investment platforms, are required to have two-factor authentication. On the question of privacy, you should look for the same kind of privacy disclosures on a robo investment platforms as you expect from other financial services companies. In the United States, privacy protections are catching up to other countries'. The robo platforms aren't great. Neither is your bank.

There's no way for you, as a consumer, to evaluate the security practices of companies, but there are a few commonsense ways to think about cybersecurity. Older, legacy companies with complicated systems are more vulnerable to attacks because software systems are most vulnerable at the places where they intersect with other software systems. Newer finance companies, such as the robo investment platforms, have an advantage at the present.

Relative Returns: How to Check Up on Your Approach

There is a straightforward way to evaluate how well you and your robo investment platform are doing. You can also use this approach, if you're not on a robo investment platform, to evaluate your traditional investment advisor, your own DIY performance with a brokerage service or trading app, or a target-date fund. To use this method, you need to understand the concept of relative returns. And in order to understand the concept, you'll need to let go of one last misconception.

Misconception #18: If you are earning high returns, you're doing great.

The truth is more complicated. If you are enmeshed in this particular misconception, you won't periodically evaluate what you're doing, which is crucial no matter what kind of investing approach you decide on. You could be caught flat if the market turns down, because you're taking too much risk. Or you could be giving away returns that you might have earned.

In Chapter 1, we wrote about how investing is like climbing a hill while yo-yo-ing. But not all hills have the same slope. Some are steep and some are gentle and less risky. You're less likely to stumble on a gentle slope. And the speed at which you climb is your own, determined by things such as your physical condition, whether you're traveling in a wheelchair, and the altitude. Most of the time, you need not concern yourself with how fast you're doing relative to other climbers. The important thing is making it to the top.[‡]

[‡] Whether you are motivated by the view, the sense of accomplishment, or the ice cream shop/bar at the summit.

But every once in a while, it's good to check up on your performance relative to others'. You might want to learn about other techniques to get there faster or more easily, or you might want to slow down and worry less about falling.

In the investment world, there is a way to measure your relative progress, or relative return, against other climbers on similarly shaped hills. This measurement will give you information about how well you're doing and importantly, how well your investment advisor or robo investment platform is doing. We suggest checking your returns against a good benchmark once a year.

The key is to understand which benchmark to use. It doesn't make much sense to compare your rate of climb on one of the slopes in the Smoky Mountains of Tennessee against climbers ascending Colorado's Front Range.

The most commonly used benchmark is the S&P 500, but it only works as a good benchmark if you have an all-stocks portfolio. If you're underperforming the S&P over one, five, or ten years, don't feel bad. The vast majority of professional stock managers underperform. For all the reasons we've talked about in this book, if you're trying to build your wealth by trading stocks or buying stock mutual funds, underperforming the S&P 500 is a strong signal that you should change your approach.

If you're managing a diversified portfolio (one that includes index funds of other asset classes, such as bonds, or emerging growth stocks), or having a traditional advisor manage one for you, you need different benchmarks. You could compare your performance to three options: a lesser-known benchmark called the 60/40 (you can find it on Kiplinger), a Vanguard target-date fund for people on your retirement schedule, or a robo advisor portfolio at your level of risk. An easy proxy for a multi-asset portfolio's level of risk is its percentage allocation in stocks. Remember to subtract the fees for each.

If you are using a traditional investment advisor, you will probably be *significantly* underperforming either the 60/40, a target-date fund, or a robo investment advisor's portfolio over time, simply because of the higher fees.

If you are already a client of a robo investment advisor, you can compare your portfolio's performance each year to that of the advisor's classic or basic portfolio. If you have customized your portfolio, your portfolio will most likely underperform the classic portfolio, over time. Remember, the robo investment platform is by definition statistically the most likely to yield the highest return possible for each risk level over time.

If you're outperforming the classic portfolio, you got lucky. Be aware that the outperformance is unlikely to last. Even if you have a diversified portfolio, you can compare your returns to the S&P 500, just to understand the returns you're giving up by taking less risk. The downside of your decision to lower your risk by investing in more than one asset class is that you are giving up some returns over time.

The upside of your decision to lower your risk by investing in more than one asset class is that your portfolio is less volatile.

Robo investment platforms should all generate nearly the same pretax returns on their classic or basic portfolios. Most of them use similar asset classes and mix them in similar ways. When it comes to the after-tax, after-fee return, the difference between them boils down to how much tax savings they generate.

The concept of relative returns is hard for people to understand. They forget to subtract fees, or they forget, in hindsight, that part of what they were striving for was less risk. Lower risk, less volatility, has a real value. The biggest reasons to engage in this kind of benchmarking once a year is to engage your critical thinking skills on these two fundamental questions: Is your after-tax, after-fee saving and investing regime enough to meet your financial goals? Are you investing with the least amount of risk possible?

Key Takeaways in This Chapter

1. There are 14 solid robo investment platforms in the market as of the summer of 2023. Check them out against the feature list we provided in this chapter.
2. Look for a company that aligns with your values, in that it has taken a low-fee approach and is transparent.
3. Consider how well your investing approach is working for you at least once a year by benchmarking.

Chapter Fifteen

Now I've Finished the Book and So What?

~

By AUTOMATING PORTFOLIO DESIGN and management, a handful of robo investment platforms have put high-quality investment advice in reach of millions of people for low cost and with a low account minimum. In this book, we outlined a simple approach to using these platforms:

- Save and invest regularly over the long term;
- Trust the diversified portfolios on the platforms;

- Understand and stick to low-fee investments;
- Seize chances to minimize your taxes;
- Understand your own relationship with money so that you set good financial goals;
- Stay the course through market volatility;
- Play a little. If you like, use a small percentage of your portfolio to play by investing in individual stocks or narrowly focused ETFs, but avoid the temptations of new, unproven investment ideas;
- Check up on your approach and your platform by using financial planning tools and by looking critically at your level of risk and your returns at least once a year.

If you follow this approach on a robo investment platform, you can make impressive returns in your sleep. Most people need to give up the idea that if they work enough and are smart enough, they can beat the market. The idea that an individual can consistently beat the market runs counter to all the research and evidence of the past century of investing: you cannot beat the collective intelligence and price-setting power of today's market. Our approach, and the philosophy of robo investing, is different: You can do well if you relax and control what you can control: diversify, invest for the long term, and keep your fees and taxes low.

In Chapter 1, we wrote that you'd need to be open to unlearning what you thought you knew about investing.

Much about investing is counterintuitive, and much is a narrative that has been sold to you by large financial services companies. Investing can be easy, but you need to think critically about investment services people and companies aim to sell you. Remember: cheap is good, but free is suspect.

In this *Little Book*, we also debunked 18 misconceptions about investing. Here they are:

Misconception #1: Investing means buying individual stocks.

If you believe this, you will be putting yourself at unnecessary financial risk and probably pay too much in fees and taxes, to boot. Here's a simple-and-true definition of investing, a foundation to build on: investing is the art of driving an increase in your net worth over the long term, meaning more than three years. Today, that means buying low-cost index funds that represent a mixture of asset classes with their own risk/reward profiles.

Misconception #2: If you use an investment company, it's working for you.

Investment companies and professionals may or may not be working for you. Some companies, including those that identify themselves as robo investment platforms or robo advisors are fiduciaries. That means they are required by regulation to act in your best interest and to disclose conflicts of interest. Other investment companies are regulated differently and are held to lower legal standards that enable them to sell high-priced products and services even when there are lower-priced versions available. Always check, and always seek fiduciary advice.

Misconception #3: You, a typical investor, can beat the market.

Misconception #4: You can beat the market over the long term by recognizing great buys in individual stocks or funds.

Misconception #5: You can beat the market by figuring out which way it is heading and "timing" the market.

One hundred years of research and Nobel Prize–winning math and science has demonstrated that investors cannot beat the market consistently. The market is too complicated, and humans are too fallible. You might win, by luck, in the short term, with the purchase of an individual stock or ETF, but do not mistake this for skill that can be extended to a long-term strategy. You also cannot time the market by selling before it goes down or buying when it turns up. In fact, investors' attempts to time the market are responsible for lots of underperformance. Over the 30 years during 1993–2022, the average equity fund investor underperformed the S&P 500 by as much as 2.8% per year, according to the research firm Dalbar.[1] An investor who missed the S&P 500's 10 best days in each decade since 1930 would have earned a total return of 28%. The investor who held steady through the ups and downs would have earned 17,715%.[2]

You cannot beat the market, but you can match the impressive returns of the stock market over time with a diversified, low-fee portfolio.

Misconception #6: A bear market will kill you.

Bear markets can hurt, but if you have a diversified portfolio, they won't kill you. There have been about 12 bear markets (declines of 20% or more) since 1965. The average time to recover from the bear markets of 1965–2019 was 654 days, or less than two years.[3] If you had owned an S&P 500 index fund, which holds the largest 500 stocks in the US stock market, in 2008 and 2022, the two worst bear-market years in the last 20 years, you would have lost 37% in 2008 and 18% in 2022. It certainly hurts to lose 37% or 18% in a single year, but your portfolio will not be wiped out.

Misconception #7: You're not paying investment fees, or they're so small they don't make a difference anyway.

All kinds of financial services companies charge fees. They look small because they are often expressed as a percent, such as 1% or 0.25%. On a 30-year retirement portfolio worth $100,000 to start, and growing at 7% a year, the difference between 1% (the fee charged by a traditional financial advisor) and 0.25% (a typical robo investment platform fee) could be as much as $136,000. Low fees are the predictor of good returns for a fund and your portfolio.

But fees in the financial services industry are famously like a whack-a-mole game. If you're not paying them in one area, chances are good you're paying more than you should be for something else. On your robo investment platform, look for a low advisory fee (under 0.35%), low fund fees (expense ratios under 0.15%), and any hidden fees (such as for account transfers, which can be in the hundreds of dollars).

Misconception #8: You don't pay taxes on money you make from investing.

You pay taxes on dividends from stocks and bonds in the year the dividends are paid. When you sell an investment, you pay taxes on the realized capital gain. (You don't pay taxes if the investment goes down in value.) The capital gains tax rate is lower, especially if you've held an investment for at least a year.

The government offers extremely valuable incentives to invest for retirement: many kinds of retirement plans are tax-free or tax-deferred. Generally, pushing off taxes into the future is advantageous if you leave the money you saved on taxes to grow in the market.

Robo investment platforms offer a service that previously was available only to the wealthy. Tax-loss harvesting makes the most of losses in a diversified portfolio to give most investors a $3,000 deduction to write off against their annual income tax. Larger and more volatile portfolios can get a bigger benefit.

Misconception #9: Investing is only for wealthy white men.

Since the 1970s, a movement to make investing accessible for everyone brought fund fees and trading commissions down. Robo investment platforms are the next wave of this movement: by lowering fees and account minimums, they democratized high-quality investment advice. Robo investment platforms have also made diversified investing (which is lower risk) more accessible. At the same time, our economy has changed so that many more people are responsible for their own retirements and for saving higher amounts to buy houses. Some research suggests that women are **better** investors than men because they listen to advice more!

Misconception #10: People make rational decisions with their money.

A growing body of research and theory demonstrates how much our emotions affect our attitudes and decisions about money. In the behavioral economics classic *Thinking, Fast and Slow*, Daniel Kahneman outlines the two systems of thinking that go on in our human brains: System 1, which is fast and intuitive, and System 2, which is slow and effortful: critical thinking. To engage System 2 when you are faced with a financial decision, slow down and do the math to look at your options. This will help you better frame your decisions and recognize if your emotions are affecting your judgment.

Misconception #11: Investing should be exciting, like day-trading or investing early in a new trend.

From day to day, investing well on a robo platform should, for the most part, be boring. Our approach calls for you to be high on conscientiousness, low on neuroticism, and low-to-medium on novelty. As robo investment platforms matured, they added more investment services, enabling you to vary your portfolio or to trade individual stocks or ETFs. Trading individual stocks and ETFs is akin to gambling or playing. Play the market if it gives you pleasure, but do so with less than 2–5% of your portfolio.

Misconception #12: The key to saving (the precursor to investing) is being frugal.

Most people find it easier to earn more than to spend less. Focus on maximizing your income, especially when you're young. You also need to live below your means. Automate deductions from your bank account into your investment accounts. And remember to live for the present and budget for some joys and luxuries. As when you are dieting, the key to maintaining a long-term strategy is giving yourself the latitude to splurge sometimes.

Misconception #13: You should max out your risk profile as an investor, to earn the highest returns possible.

Some investors, especially small and new investors, overestimate their risk tolerance on a robo investment platform. They can be caught short. They yank their money out when the market takes a turn downward because they panic. Some investors withdraw money because they find themselves in need of money just at the time the market turns down.

Cashing out when the market turns down is one of investors' worst mistakes.

Think carefully about how much money you need in the next three years. Keep that money in cash (for money needed within one year) or low-risk bonds (for money needed in one to three years). After that, think about what amount of money you can afford to lose in a downturn at the worst possible time. It's reasonable to assume that your portfolio won't drop more than 50%, based on the single worst bear market in modern history.

One formula to make sure you have enough excess cash is your emergency savings plus 50% of your invested portfolio. If that's enough for you to get through the worst three to five years of your financial life, you have enough of a cushion to shift up to a high-risk portfolio, on a robo investment platform.

Misconception #14: Investing is all about money.

Investing is also about time. As you make investing decisions, factor in the long-term effects of compounding, inflation, interest payments on debt, and tax efficiency. Whenever possible, turn time into your ally by leaving your money in the market, pushing taxes into the future, and when you need to borrow, keeping interest rates as low as possible.

Misconception #15: Volatile times are a bad time to invest.

Regular investing through a volatile market has been shown to produce higher returns than regular investing in steadily rising markets.

Misconception #16: A Do-It-Yourself investment strategy is just as good as a robo investment platform.

Optimal investing requires superhuman discipline to rebalance portfolios, find ways to lower your taxes, and keep up with the latest research and innovation. A robo investment platform can do those things; a DIY investor can't. But if you truly love DIY investing, the strong chance you will underperform might be OK for you.

Misconception #17: It's impossible to pick between robo investment platforms.

You can consider the companies' values, compare features, look at the user interfaces to see which ones you prefer, and look at the regulatory history to see whether and how much their services have been fined.

Misconception #18: If you're earning high returns you're doing great.

You can check up on your robo investment platform (or any investment approach) after you understand the concept of relative returns. If the market is skyrocketing, are your returns keeping up? And if it's falling, is your diversified approach paying off in lower volatility? If you have an all-stock portfolio, look at your returns relative to the S&P 500. If you have a diversified portfolio, look at your returns relative to the basic diversified portfolio of 60% stocks/40% bonds. (A search on Google or ChatGPT will give you access to those benchmarks.)

Explanations of Investing

Partway through writing this book, we sent drafts to professional and everyday investors to figure out whether we were getting our points across. Shortly thereafter, Qian's sister sent back a note saying that she was excited to open an account on a robo investment platform after years of trying to do DIY index investing. Her note caught Qian by surprise, because she had so often mentioned robo investing to her sister over the years. That showed us: there's no substitute for the depth that a book can bring to the topic of robo investing.

Remember Elizabeth's friend Jodi in Chapter 1? Trying to explain investing to many friends over the years hooked Elizabeth on the question "Where to begin?" to explain robo investing's merit for the majority of individual investors, including Jodi, Qian's sister, and you. We hope our explanation in this book resonates with you.

Now you've finished the book and might ask, "So what?" First, thank you for reading. Second, congratulations on investing in yourself with knowledge. Last but not least, get started to invest your money.

If you don't have a robo investing account yet, we suggest starting with a small cash account, to familiarize yourself with the user interface. You can also open a small taxable investment account (if you pick a platform with a low minimum) to see whether you like the financial planning tools and feel confident in the portfolio the platform builds for you. You can even try two or three (more than three is an overkill) robo platforms, each with a small amount of money.

Pick a robo platform and move on from there. Remember the priorities: an emergency savings account and making sure you are saving enough for retirement.

It takes about a few minutes to sign up and start the process to fund an account, either on a website or a smartphone app. You'll need your bank account number so you can set up a transfer. It's as easy as using Venmo or PayPal.

If you already have a robo investing account, we hope this book has given you information that makes you more confident so you can use the platform most effectively. We also hope that letting go of some of the day-to-day challenges of investing gives you more time to do what you love. Check in with your accounts as often as you like but at least a few times a year. Pass the book along to someone who might benefit from robo investing.

After the robo investment platform is making you enough money (in your sleep) for your own financial security, and for you to take care of your family, please consider giving back. Donate to your community and causes you believe in. That's the ultimate happiness money can buy.

Key Takeaways in This Chapter

1. Better late than never!
2. Get started!

Four Biggest Mistakes Investors Make

1. Not being diversified enough;
2. Trying to beat the market by trading or timing;
3. Seeking excitement through investing;
4. Making financial decisions by fear.

References

Introduction

1. Barbara Friedberg, "Top-10 Robo-Advisors By Assets Under Management," *Forbes*, July 9, 2022, https://www.forbes.com/advisor/investing/top-robo-advisors-by-aum/.

Chapter One: Make Investing Work for You

1. Moise, Imani, "Bond Investing Gets the Robo-Adviser Treatment," *The Wall Street Journal*, June 7, 2023, https://www.wsj.com/articles/buying-bonds-is-hard-heres-a-way-to-let-a-robot-do-it-70a4587b.
2. Employee Benefit Research Institute and Greenwald Research, "2023 Retirement Confidence Survey," *Employee Benefit Research Institute*, April 27, 2023, https://www.ebri.org/docs/default-source/rcs/2023-rcs/2023-rcs-short-report.pdf.
3. Damodaran, Aswath, "Historical Returns on Stocks, Bonds and Bills: 1928–2022," January 2023, https://pages.stern.nyu.edu/~adamodar/New_Home_Page/datafile/histretSP.html.

4. Israel, Spencer, "The Number of Companies Publicly Traded in the US Is Shrinking—Or Is It?," *MarketWatch*, October 30, 2020, https://www.marketwatch.com/story/the-number-of-companies-publicly-traded-in-the-us-is-shrinkingor-is-it-2020-10-30.

Chapter Two: A Brief History of Indexing and Robo Investing

1. Edwards, Tim, Anu R. Ganti, Craig J. Lazzara, Joe Nelesen, and Davide Di Gioia, "SPIVA® U.S. Scorecard," *S&P Dow Jones Indices*, 2023, https://www.spglobal.com/spdji/en/documents/spiva/spiva-us-year-end-2022.pdf.

2. Sloan, Allan, "'The Democratization of Investing': Index Funds Officially Overtake Active Managers," *Yahoo Finance*, May 22, 2022, https://news.yahoo.com/index-fund-assets-exceed-active-fund-assets-120639243.html.

3. Kauflin, Jeff, and Antoine Gara, "The Inside Story of Robinhood's Billionaire Founders, Option Kid Cowboys and The Wall Street Sharks That Feed on Them," *Forbes*, August 19, 2020, https://www.forbes.com/sites/jeffkauflin/2020/08/19/the-inside-story-of-robinhoods-billionaire-founders-option-kid-cowboys-and-the-wall-street-sharks-that-feed-on-them.

4. The Securities and Exchange Commission, "SEC Charges Robinhood Financial With Misleading Customers About Revenue Sources and Failing to Satisfy Duty of Best Execution," December 17, 2020, https://www.sec.gov/news/press-release/2020-321.

5. de la Merced, Michael J., and Erin Griffith, "Robinhood Is Fined $70 Million over Misleading Customers and System Outages," June 30, 2021, https://www.nytimes.com/2021/06/30/technology/robinhood-fined-misleading-customers.html.

6. Nishant, Niket, "Robinhood's Crypto Arm Fined $30 Mln by New York State's Financial Regulator," *Reuters*, August 2, 2022, https://www.reuters.com/business/robinhoods-crypto-arm-fined-30-mln-by-new-york-states-financial-regulator-2022-08-02/.

Chapter Three: The Philosophy of Robo Investment Advice: Avoid the Gimmicks, Embrace the Science

1. Routley, Nick, "This Is How Many Humans Have Ever Existed, According to Researchers," *World Economic Forum*, April 4, 2022, https://www.weforum.org/agenda/2022/04/quantifying-human-existence/.

2. Sommer, Jeff, "Mutual Funds That Consistently Beat the Market? Not One of 2,132," December 2, 2022, https://www.nytimes.com/2022/12/02/business/stock-market-index-funds.html.

3. Bureau of Labor Statistics, "CPI Inflation Calculator," 2023, https://www.bls.gov/data/inflation_calculator.htm.

4. Fink, Larry, and David Rubinstein, Aspen Ideas Festival, June 26, 2023.

5. Stevens, Pippa, "This Chart Shows Why Investors Should Never Try to Time the Stock Market," *CNBC*, March 24, 2021, https://www.cnbc.com/2021/03/24/this-chart-shows-why-investors-should-never-try-to-time-the-stock-market.html.

Chapter Four: Diversify and De-risk Investments

1. Rachleff, Andy, "There's No Need to Fear a Bear Market," March 16, 2020, https://www.wealthfront.com/blog/theres-no-need-to-fear-a-bear-market/.

2. Kloepfer, Jay, "The Callan Periodic Table of Investment Returns: Year-End 2022," *Callan Institute,* 2023, https://www.callan.com/research/2022-classic-periodic-table.

3. Arnott, Amy, "Why Rebalancing (Almost Always) Pays Off," *Morningstar*, July 6, 2020, https://www.morningstar.com/markets/why-rebalancing-almost-always-pays-off.

4. Coleman, Murray, "Dalbar QAIB 2023: Investors Are Still Their Own Worst Enemies," April 3, 2023, https://www.ifa.com/articles/dalbar_2016_qaib_investors_still_their_worst_enemy.

5. Global Asset Allocation Strategy Team, "The Perils of Trying to Time Volatile Markets," *Wells Fargo Investment Institute*, September 14, 2022, https://www.wellsfargo.com/investment-institute/sr-perils-time-volatile-markets/.

Chapter Five: Increase Your Return over Time with Lower Fees

1. Arnott, Amy, "Are You Leaving Money on the Table From Your Funds' Returns?," *Morningstar*, July 12, 2022, https://www.morningstar.com/funds/are-you-leaving-money-table-your-funds-returns.

2. Constantijn, W.A. Panis, and Michael J. Brien, "Characteristics and Performance of Target Date Funds in the United States," Department of Labor, September 19, 2017, https://www.dol.gov/sites/dolgov/files/EBSA/researchers/analysis/retirement/characteristics-and-performance-of-target-date-funds-in-the-united-states.pdf.

Chapter Six: Lower Tax Bills

1. Bureau of Labor Statistics, "Retirement Plans for Workers in Private Industry and State and Local Government in 2022," *Bureau of Labor Statistics' The Economics Daily*, February 1, 2023, https://www.bls.gov/

opub/ted/2023/retirement-plans-for-workers-in-private-industry-and-state-and-local-government-in-2022.htm.

2. Hanlon, Seth, and Nick Buffie, "The Forbes 400 Pay Lower Tax Rates than Many Ordinary Americans," *The Center for American Progress*, October 7, 2021, https://www.americanprogress.org/article/forbes-400-pay-lower-tax-rates-many-ordinary-americans/.

3. The Wealthfront Team, "Tax-Loss Harvesting 101," April 22, 2021, https://www.wealthfront.com/blog/tax-loss-harvesting-101/.

Chapter Seven: Technology Brings It Home

1. Barber, Brad M., and Terrance Odean, "Boys Will Be Boys: Gender, Overconfidence, and Common Stock Investment," *Quarterly Journal of Economics*, April 20, 2000, https://papers.ssrn.com/sol3/papers.cfm?abstract_id=219240.

2. Bhutta, Neil, Andrew C. Chang, Lisa J. Dettling, and Joanne W. Hsu, "Disparities in Wealth by Race and Ethnicity in the 2019 Survey of Consumer Finances," Federal Reserve, September 28, 2020, https://www.federalreserve.gov/econres/notes/feds-notes/disparities-in-wealth-by-race-and-ethnicity-in-the-2019-survey-of-consumer-finances-20200928.html.

Chapter Eight: Be Self-Aware about Money

1. Barber, Brad M., and Terrance Odean, "Boys Will Be Boys: Gender, Overconfidence, and Common Stock Investment," *Quarterly Journal of Economics*, April 20, 2000, https://papers.ssrn.com/sol3/papers.cfm?abstract_id=219240.

Chapter Nine: Investing Is Dating for the Long Term

1. Curry, Shannon, and Lex Fridman, "Shannon Curry: Johnny Depp & Amber Heard Trial, Marriage, Dating & Love," *Lex Fridman Podcast*, 2023, https://lexfridman.com/shannon-curry/.

2. Yaffe-Bellany, David, "Embattled Crypto Exchange FTX Files for Bankruptcy," November 11, 2022, https://www.nytimes.com/2022/11/11/business/ftx-bankruptcy.html.

3. Dress, Brad, "Tom Brady, Other Celebrities Named in Class-Action Lawsuit Filed against Cryptocurrency Exchange FTX," *The Hill*, November 16, 2022, https://thehill.com/homenews/3738057-tom-brady-other-celebrities-named-in-class-action-lawsuit-filed-against-cryptocurrency-exchange-ftx/.

4. DeVon, Cheyenne, "Bitcoin Lost over 60% of Its Value in 2022—Here's How Much 6 Other Popular Cryptocurrencies Lost," December 23, 2022, https://www.cnbc.com/2022/12/23/bitcoin-lost-over-60-percent-of-its-value-in-2022.html.

5. D'Acunto, Francesco, Nagpurnanand Prabhala, and Alberto G. Rossi, "The Promises and Pitfalls of Robo-Advising," *The Review of Financial Studies*, April 4, 2019, https://academic.oup.com/rfs/article/32/5/1983/5427774.

Chapter Ten: Budgeting and Wealth Building

1. Knueven, Liz, and Sophia Acevedo, "The Average American Savings Balance by Age, Household Size, and Education Level," *Business Insider*, November 17, 2022, https://www.businessinsider.com/personal-finance/average-american-savings.

2. NerdWallet, *Monthly 50/30/20 Budget Calculator* (NerdWallet, 2022), https://www.nerdwallet.com/article/finance/nerdwallet-budget-calculator.

3. Lisa, Andrew, "What Is the Average Social Security Benefit at Every Age?," *Yahoo Finance*, August 26, 2023, https://finance.yahoo.com/news/average-social-security-benefit-every-120016509.html.
4. Pension Rights Center, "Income from Pensions," November 28, 2022, https://pensionrights.org/resource/income-from-pensions/.

Chapter Eleven: Understand Risk and Pick the Right Risk Tolerance

1. Zell, Ethan, Jason E. Strickhouser, Constantine Sedikides, and Mark D. Alicke, "The Better-than-Average Effect in Comparative Self-Evaluation: A Comprehensive Review and Meta-Analysis," *Psychological Bulletin*, February 2020, https://pubmed.ncbi.nlm.nih.gov/31789535/.
2. Killingsworth, Matthew A., Daniel Kahneman, and Barbara Mellers, "Income and Emotional Well-Being: A Conflict Resolved," *PNAS*, March 1, 2023, https://www.pnas.org/doi/10.1073/pnas.2208661120.

Chapter Twelve: Live for the Present, Invest for the Future

1. The Federal Reserve, "Report on the Economic Well-Being of U.S. Households in 2022," May 2023, https://www.federalreserve.gov/publications/2023-economic-well-being-of-us-households-in-2022-executive-summary.htm.
2. Pasquini, Giancarlo, and Scott Keeter, "At Least Four-in-Ten U.S. Adults Have Faced High Levels of Psychological Distress during COVID-19 Pandemic," Pew Research Center, December 12, 2022, https://www.pewresearch.org/short-reads/2022/12/12/at-least-four-in-ten-u-s-adults-have-faced-high-levels-of-psychological-distress-during-covid-19-pandemic/.

3. Malkiel, Burton G., "What You Should Do in Volatile and Uncertain Markets," August 24, 2015, https://www.wealthfront.com/blog/volatile-uncertain-markets/.

Chapter Thirteen: Is a Robo Investment Platform Right for You?

1. Egan, Matt, "Robinhood Settles Lawsuit over 20-Year-Old Trader Who Died by Suicide," *CNN*, July 1, 2021, https://www.cnn.com/2021/07/01/business/robinhood-lawsuit-suicide-settlement/index.html.

Chapter Fourteen: Find the Right Platform

1. Benson, Alana, "NerdWallet," *12 Best Robo-Advisors of August 2023* (blog), August 23, 2023, https://www.nerdwallet.com/best/investing/robo-advisors.

Chapter Fifteen: Now I've Finished the Book and So What?

1. Coleman, Murray, "Dalbar QAIB 2023: Investors Are Still Their Own Worst Enemies," May 11, 2017, https://itsyourmoneyandestate.org/wp-content/uploads/2023/05/Dalbar-QAIB-2023-Investors-are-Still-Their-Own-Worst-Enemies.pdf.

2. Stevens, Pippa, "This Chart Shows Why Investors Should Never Try to Time the Stock Market," *CNBC*, March 24, 2021, https://www.cnbc.com/2021/03/24/this-chart-shows-why-investors-should-never-try-to-time-the-stock-market.html.

3. Rachleff, Andy, "There's No Need to Fear a Bear Market," March 16, 2020, https://www.wealthfront.com/blog/theres-no-need-to-fear-a-bear-market/.

About the Authors

Elizabeth Macbride (Washington, DC) is an award-winning international journalist, author, and advocate for an equitable economy. She has held fellowships at MIT and Georgetown University and was on the start-up team at Wealthfront. Her work has been published in *MIT Tech Review*, *The Washington Post*, and Atlantic.com. A single mom and a military brat, she has devoted her career to being a voice for the middle class.

Back in 2011, Elizabeth was feeling decidedly disillusioned with traditional Wall Street firms. As an editor for a business newspaper in New York City, she had covered the 2008–09 financial crisis. Everyday investors, including Elizabeth, had taken hits on their retirement savings while big companies got bailouts. On a trip to California, she met

Andy Rachleff, cofounder of Wealthfront, at a backyard party for investment advisors, where he was gathering intel for the company he was launching.

From that meeting, she became Wealthfront's first editor and played a key role in developing the content, language, and voice that launched the robo advice movement.

Qian Liu (San Francisco, California) is an executive in the fintech industry. Her belief in the importance of financial security to everyone and the power of technology led her to build a career in fintech. She's one of the hidden figures of the movement over the last 15 years to bring high-quality financial services to everyone via technology.

Since 2018 Qian has been serving as the chief data officer at Guideline, a leader in the retirement industry in providing low-cost and easy-to-use 401(k) plans to small businesses and their workers via software. Between 2016 and 2018 Qian was the head of data at GoFundMe, the biggest social fundraising platform, which raised $5 billion from 50 million donors to worthy causes. Before that, Qian worked at Wealthfront between 2009 and 2015, as a key member of the company's founding team and later as the director of research. Elizabeth and Qian met as colleagues on the earliest days of Wealthfront, after Andy Rachleff recruited Qian from the University of Pennsylvania. She built the first versions of a number of Wealthfront's automated investment